The Complete Ketogenic Diet Cookbook for Beginners

Easy Keto Low-Carb Recipes for Weight Loss and Healthy Living (Plus a 30-Day Meal Plan)

By

Dr. Sara Michaels

Copyright © 2024 by Dr Sara Michaels. All Right Reserved.

No part of this publication may be reproduced, distributed, or transmitted in any form or by any means, including photocopying, recording, or other electronic or mechanical methods, or by any information storage and retrieval system without the prior written permission of the publisher, except in the case of very brief quotations embodied in critical reviews and certain other non-commercial uses permitted by copyright law.

TABLE OF CONTENT

What is the ketogenic diet

Different Types of Ketogenic Diets

HOW THE KETO DIET WORKS

Benefits Of A Ketogenic Diet

Things to Eat When On a Keto Diet

Foods to eat When on a ketogenic diet:

Foods To Avoid When On The Keto Diet

HEALTHY FAT SOURCES FOR THE KETO DIET

SHOPPING LIST WHEN ON A KETO DIST

30 DAYS MEAL PLAN

BREAKFAST RECIPES

- Chocoholic granola
- Herb Chicken Sausages With Braised Bok Choy
- Avocado Breakfast Muffins
- Buffalo chicken breakfast muffins
- Prosciutto biscuits

Salmon bacon rolls with dipping sauce

Pumpkin spice latte overnight "oats."

Keto Coffee Recipe

Rocket fuel hot chocolate

Cross-country scrambler

Full meal deal

Liver sausages & onions

Eggs benedict

Pepper sausage fry

Keto breakfast pudding

Something different breakfast Sammy

Mug biscuit

All day any day hash

Indian masala omelet

Sticky wrapped eggs

Coffee shake

Super breakfast combo

Delicious Coconut Flour Waffles

Keto Cream Cheese Pancakes

Yummy Avocado And Salmon Breakfast Boats

Healthy Vegetable Breakfast Hash

- Sausage Casserole with Vegetables
- Breakfast Tacos
- Keto Lemon Muffins With Poppy Seeds
- Cheddar And Bacon Omelets With Chives
- Salted Caramel Cereal With Pork Rinds
- Pumpkin Bread
- Red Chocolate Doughnuts
- Brownie Muffins For Ketoheads
- Cheddar Scrambled Eggs With Spinach
- Sausage And Bacon Bite Sized Breakfasts
- Versatile Oopsie Rolls
- Keto Crepes With Blueberries
- Italian Sausage And Egg Scramble
- Keto Cheddar and Sage Waffle
- Breakfast Burgers
- Keto Casserole For Breakfast
- Peanut Butter Muffins With Chocolate Chips
- Keto Oatmeal

- Keto Green Smoothie
- Carrot Muffins
- Quick Keto Scramble
- Savory Delicious Bacon Muffins
- Keto Banana Pancake
- Little Red Chocolate Cakes
- Keto French Toast

Lunch Recipes
- Keto Chicken Salad
- Keto Tacos
- Spicy Cauliflower Soup
- Keto Mexican Rice w/ Chorizo
- Zucchini Noodles w/ Pesto
- Keto Deviled Eggs
- Keto Cashew Chicken
- Shrimp Tacos w/ Mango Avocado Salsa
- Paleo Sushi Rolls
- Keto Bread
- Keto Meatballs
- Easy chopped salad
- Chili-lime chicken bowls

- Salmon salad cups
- Steak-fried cups
- Antipasto Salad
- German no-tato salad
- Broccoli Ginger Soup
- Sauerkraut Soup
- Zucchini Boats
- Keto Flat Bread
- Keto Stromboli
- Tuna Bites With Avocado
- Keto Chicken Sandwich
- Keto Green Salad
- Easy Egg Soup
- Original Keto Stuffed Hot Dogs
- Original Nasi Lemak
- Mug Cake With Jalapeño
- Keto Sausage And Pepper Soup
- Original Squash Lasagna
- Fresh Keto Sandwich
- Chili Soup
- Cauliflower Rice With Chicken

- Chicken Nuggets For Keto Nuts
- Zucchini Keto Wraps
- Keto Casserole With Chicken And Bacon
- Cauliflower Soup With Bacon And Cheddar
- Mexican-Style Casserole With Spinach
- Chicken Salad
- Almond Pizza
- Keto Chicken Thighs
- Keto Pork Stew
- Bbq Chicken Soup
- Keto Enchilada Soup
- Keto Caprese Salad
- Grilled Cheese Sandwich
- Vegetarian Curry
- Asian Salad

DINNER RECIPES

- Noodles & glazed salmon
- Crispy thighs & mash
- Scallops & Mozza broccoli mash
- Cream of mushroom-stuffed chicken

- Bbq beef & slaw
- Crispy pork with lemon-thyme cauli rice
- Salmon & kale
- One-pot porky kale
- Creamy spinach zucchini boats
- Original Keto Burger with Portobello Bun
- My favourite creamy pesto chicken
- Keto Pork Chops
- Pork Hock
- Meatballs With Bacon And Cheese
- Keto Crisp Pizza
- Bacon Wrapped Chicken
- Little Portobello Pizza
- Keto Broccoli Soup
- Cheddar Biscuits
- Bacon Wrap
- Sausage & Cabbage Skillet Melt
- Spaghetti Squash With Meat Sauce
- Keto Chicken Tikka Masala
- Keto Guacamole

- Keto Parmesan Chicken
- Cheesy Bacon Brussels Sprouts
- Creamy Chicken
- LOW CARB CHICKEN NUGGETS
- Cheeseburger Soup With Bacon
- Sushie!
- Keto Salad With Radish And Asparagus
- Kung Pao Chicken
- Keto Totchos
- Stuffed Burgers
- PORK PIES
- Keto Thai Zoodles
- Chicken Satay
- Stuffed Peppers
- Coconut Shrimp
- Glazed Salmon
- Conclusion

What is the ketogenic diet

The ketogenic diet is a diet that is rich in fat, moderate in protein, and low in carbohydrates. Originally developed to treat children with epileptic seizures, researchers found that other adults could benefit from the ketogenic diet as well.

The ketogenic diet aims to bring your body into the metabolic state of ketosis, in which it uses fat as its primary energy source instead of sugar from carbohydrates. With ketosis, your body functions on ketones, which are molecules that are generated from the breakdown of the fat in your diet or the fat stored in your body.

To establish and maintain ketosis, most people must reduce their total intake of carbohydrates to 20-50 grams each day. The macronutrient ranges for the ketogenic diet typically consist of 20%

from proteins, 5% from carbs, and 75% from fat. Most people use breath, blood, or urine tests to measure the amount of ketone generation in their bodies.

The popular South Beach diet from long ago was comparable to the ketogenic diet. This diet is low in carbohydrates and high in fat, with the goal of putting your body into ketosis so it can burn fat more quickly. What is the state of ketosis? Ketosis occurs when your body does not have enough glucose to burn energy, so it starts burning fat, generating an accumulation of ketones in the body. Most of the time, starch or sugar provide adequate ketone (that is, carbs) for humans. However, these nutrients are not included in the ketogenic diet, which forces the body to burn fat instead of glucose when it is low on them.

Under the keto diet, you will increase your fat intake to a significantly higher level (up to 65% of your daily macronutrient intake) and drastically reduce your carbohydrate intake (no more than 30 g or nearly 0 g per day). This is intended to induce ketosis in your body. Research confirms that ketosis makes the body use fat for energy. You should be shredded if you use your glycogen and carbs as fuel first and then use fat.

Many people think that the ketogenic diet is a fantastic substitute for losing weight. It's a completely different diet, allowing the person following it to consume foods they wouldn't normally include in their diet.

Thus, the ketogenic diet, often known as the low-carbohydrate, high-fat diet, is based on this principle. There aren't many diets that allow you to eat a lot of bacon and eggs in the morning, chicken wings for lunch, and broccoli and steak in the evening. Many may find that to be unbelievable. This is a terrific day to eat on the diet, and you've done a perfect job of following the plan of action with that meal.

Your body enters a state or phase of ketosis when you consume very little in the way of carbohydrates. This indicates that fat is used by the body as fuel. What is the required amount of carbohydrates to enter ketosis? It varies, of course, from person to person, but generally speaking, it's safe to keep net carbs under 25. In the "induction phase," when you enter ketosis, many recommend staying below 10 net carbohydrates.

Here's a brief explanation of net carbs in case you're unfamiliar with the term or want to clarify what it implies. The quantity of carbohydrates you eat minus the amount of dietary fiber is what's known as net carbohydrates. Therefore, your daily net carbohydrate count would be 22 if you consumed 35 grams of net carbohydrates and 13 grams of dietary fiber.

There are additional advantages to the ketogenic diet in addition to weight loss, such as reduced appetite, enhanced mental clarity, and increased energy.

When you follow a ketogenic diet, one thing to be concerned about is "keto flu." It can be challenging for this, although not everyone has this experience. You may experience a headache and a lethargic feeling that is out of the ordinary. If that's how you feel, make sure you get enough rest and water to help you through.

Different Types of Ketogenic Diets

Because the keto diet differs slightly from the food that most people are familiar with, it may be quite difficult to stick to over time. As a result, there are now many different types of ketogenic diets available, ranging from extremely restrictive to fairly forgiving. The following explains the many ketogenic diet types:\

Clean Keto Diet

The clean keto diet focuses mostly on minimally processed whole foods, such as high-quality meat and/or protein, a variety of healthy fats and oils, a large number of non-starchy vegetables, herbs, spice broth, and probiotic items.

Keto-cycling or carb-cycling

Eating low-carbohydrate foods for the majority of the week while purposefully consuming more carbohydrates on one or two days to replenish glycogen levels and avoid adverse effects like exhaustion is known as keto or carb cycling.

Modified keto diet

A modified keto diet provides greater flexibility and a wider variety of foods because it contains marginally more protein and carbs than a typical keto diet. One drawback is that maintaining ketosis while adhering to a modified plan might not be simple, but for some people, this is a long-term, sustainable, and healthy eating pattern.

Ketotarian diet

A ketotarian diet is a variation of the ketogenic diet that emphasizes vegetables or seafood. For those who wish to get the benefits of keto but still like a diet high in vegetables, it is a wonderful option.

Eco-keto diet

"Eco-Keto" is a snappy term for a ketogenic diet that is kind to the environment. The vast majority of people confuse eco-keto with vegan or fully vegetable-based ketosis.

HOW THE KETO DIET WORKS

The ketogenic diet is a low-carb, high-fat eating plan. A state of ketosis, in which your body uses ketone bodies for energy rather than glucose, is the aim of the keto diet. However, how does the ketogenic diet function, and how may one enter a state of ketosis? Continue reading.

The majority of Western diets, including the traditional American diet, are primarily composed of carbs, with little amounts of protein and very little fat. The average person's body absorbs and converts carbohydrates from high-carb meals into glucose. The glucose is then delivered to the cell by insulin. When there are carbs present, the body uses glucose as its main energy source.

When Since you typically consume very little in the way of carbohydrates when following a ketogenic diet, your body must find another way to stay energy-efficient, which is where fats come into play. In the absence of carbs, the body's fatty acids are converted by the liver into ketone bodies, also known as ketones, which are used as an energy source. For those following a ketogenic diet, this state is known as ketosis. Three types of ketones are formed when fatty acids split or break down. These are:

- Acetoacetate (AcAc): This is first formed during the process of ketosis
- Acetone: This ketone is spontaneously formed as a side product of acetoacetate
- Beta-hydroxybutyric acid (BHB): This is formed and created from acetoacetate

Benefits Of the Ketogenic Diet

You can maintain your energy, mood, and cognitive focus when you adhere to a ketogenic diet and don't need to consume regular meals. Weight reduction is one of the biggest benefits of a diet that encourages the body to burn fat for energy, particularly when the diet first puts your body into a state of ketosis. But there are additional advantages if you can carefully prepare and carry out your keto diet plan.

The following are some advantages of the ketogenic diet:

1. Puts an end to counting calories

Because the ketogenic diet includes proteins and healthy fats, you won't need to track calories because you'll feel satisfied.

2. More energy.

Since you are not increasing your blood sugar levels when following the ketogenic diet, you often experience a continuous and consistent flow of keto energy rather than troughs during the day.

3. Improved mental Clarity.

Your brain, muscles, and organs receive a constant energy boost from ketones. Relatively speaking, this can improve concentration, memory, attention span, and, most importantly, learning and problem-solving skills.

4. Brain defence

According to Dr. Axe, the diet provides defense against a variety of neurodegenerative conditions, including stroke, traumatic brain injury, Parkinson's disease, and Alzheimer's disease.

5. Normal blood sugar levels.

In adults with diabetes and prediabetes, reducing blood sugar instability and insulin resistance through diets high in fat and low in carbohydrates is helpful.

Things to Eat When On a Keto Diet

Consuming large amounts of fat is referred to as going keto. On the ketogenic diet, the majority of calories come from fat, with relatively little coming from carbs and an average amount from protein. When following a ketogenic diet, the breakdown of macronutrients for the majority of people looks like this:

- *5%–10% are gotten from carbohydrates*
- *20–25% of calories come from protein*
- *70%–80% of calories come from fat*

Individuals who typically eat low-carbohydrate foods would come to understand that in order to improve their ketosis condition, they needed to eat minimal amounts of carbohydrates.

When A ketogenic diet entails eating high-fat foods like nuts, seeds, avocados, coconut oil, olive oil, and MCT oil. Moreover, you should consume grass-fed meats, premium eggs, seafood, and full-fat dairy products. Leafy greens, along with several other ketogenic vegetables like Brussels sprouts, cauliflower, and spinach, are good sources of vitamins, minerals, and fiber.

By all means, avoid sugar, starch, and grains when following a ketogenic diet. As a general guideline, limit your intake of veggies to no more than 10 grams of carbohydrates (or roughly 5 grams of net carbs) per serving. Your diet strategy should be focused on keeping your daily carbohydrate intake under 30 grams.

More importantly, don't limit your calorie consumption when on keto. One of the biggest mistakes people make while following a ketogenic diet is restricting their calorie intake, which often results in inadequate calorie intake after cutting out carbohydrates and sugar.

Foods to eat When on a ketogenic diet:

Meat

Organic and grass-fed meats are even healthier than processed meats, which are both low in carbs and keto-friendly. However, keep in mind that the ketogenic diet is low in protein and high in fat, so you won't need a lot of meat. Some people find it more difficult to enter ketosis when they consume more protein than their bodies require, particularly when they are just starting out and have significant levels of insulin resistance.

Fish

Fish and seafood are both delicious, especially fatty fish like salmon. Increase your intake of smaller fish, such as herring, sardines, and mackerel, if mercury or other pollutants are causing you concern. The best fish are generally those that have been captured in the wild, but be careful not to breed them because they contain carbs.

Eggs

Eggs: Consume them however you like—baked with butter, scrambled eggs, cooked omelettes, or any combination thereof. Purchasing organic or pastured eggs is probably the healthiest choice, although there isn't any scientific evidence to support this claim. When considering cholesterol, how many eggs can you eat? We advise against eating more than 36 eggs a day. You can, however, eat less if you'd like.

Sauces and fats

Fat must provide the bulk of the calories in a ketogenic diet. Most of it will likely come from foods that are naturally occurring, such as meat, eggs, fish, etc. It's also beneficial to use cooking fat, like butter or coconut oil, and dress salads and other dishes with a lot of olive oil. You can also enjoy mouthwatering sauces that are high in fat, such as bearnaise sauce or garlic butter.

Keto low-carb Vegetables

Vegetables are plants that grow above the ground; fresh or frozen is OK. This is the reason you should choose veggies that grow above ground, especially those that are lush and green. Favorites include avocado, cabbage, cauliflower, broccoli, and zucchini. Vegetables are one of the best ketogenic diet options for consuming good, healthy fats. Add a generous amount of olive oil to your salad, then fry it in butter. Some people even think of veggies as a way to distribute fat. They also enhance a keto meal's color, flavor, and variety.

Vegetables replace grains like rice, pasta, potatoes, and the like, so many people find that they are eating more vegetables than they were before they started the keto diet.

Keto dairy

Dairy products with high fat content When cooking, heavy cream, butter, and cheese with a high fat content are all acceptable. Milk should be avoided since it quickly accumulates sugar (15 grams of carbs per glass), while you can use a small amount when brewing coffee. Here, "sparingly" refers to how many cups you drink each day! One cup plus an inch, or a maximum of one tablespoon. But abstaining from milk entirely is preferable.

It's also critical to stay away from low-fat yogurts because they have a lot of added sugar, as well as coffee lattes, which contain roughly 18 grams of carbohydrates. Be advised that eating cheese on a daily basis while you're not hungry is a big mistake that can prevent you from losing weight.

Keto Nuts

These can be eaten in moderation, but you should exercise caution when using them as snacks because it's easy to eat more than you need to feel satisfied. Also, keep in mind that cashews are extremely high in carbs, so you can substitute macadamia or pecan nuts. When is too much keto nuts? That depends on how many carbohydrates you eat and how far along you are in your weight loss journey. It's crucial to make an effort to keep daily nut consumption to less than or equal to 1/2 cup (or 50 grams).

Berries

Berries - When following a ketogenic diet, berries in moderation are OK, especially when combined with real whipped cream—a popular keto treat.

Foods To Avoid When On The Keto Diet

People on the ketogenic diet should stay away from high-carb foods.

Grains

Carbohydrate-rich foods include cereal, rice, pasta, beer, crackers and bread. Whole-wheat pasta and the new bean-based spaghetti are likewise heavy in carbohydrates. Consider options like shirataki noodles or spiralized veggies, which contain low carbs and are a healthy alternative. Sugar-filled breakfast cereals and whole-grain cereals are high in carbohydrates and are to be avoided or used sparingly. You could theoretically eat one slice of bread per day because it typically includes about 11 grams of carbohydrates, but that would mean you would be consuming all of your carbohydrates on unhealthful foods.

Beer

On a low-carb diet, beer is OK in moderation. Dry wine and spirits are an alternative to that; however, moderation is advised while consuming alcohol.

Starchy vegetables and high-sugar fruits

Starchy vegetables should not be consumed while following a ketogenic diet since they contain more easily digested carbohydrates than fiber. These consist of potatoes, maize, beets, and sweet potatoes. Limit your consumption of high-sugar fruits, as they contain more carbohydrates and raise blood sugar levels more quickly than berries.

Juices

Fruit juices, whether organic or not, should be consumed in moderation or avoided entirely due to their high carbohydrate content, which can quickly raise blood sugar levels. Consider using water instead.

Honey, sugar, syrup of any form

Steer clear of maple syrup, honey, and sugar in any form, as they are high in carbs and lacking in nutrients.

Crackers and chips

Steer clear of processed crackers, chips, and other grain-based snack items because they are poor in fiber and heavy in carbohydrates.

Gluten-free baked products

Gluten-free does not mean carb-free. Numerous gluten-free bread loaves and muffins have about the same amount of carbs as regular baked goods. They also have very little fiber.

HEALTHY FAT SOURCES FOR THE KETO DIET

The ketogenic diet, also referred to as the "keto diet," is characterized by a low carbohydrate content, an average protein content, and a high fat content. This suggests that foods high in healthy fat content and extremely rich are the ideal ketogenic options. In contrast, 75% of the calories in a ketogenic diet come from fat, 20% come from protein, and 5% come from carbohydrates.

Full-fat Greek yogurt

Whole-fat Greek yogurt with added fat is high in protein and saturated fats. Following a ketogenic meal plan usually involves a combination of unsaturated and saturated fats; nevertheless, dieticians believe that meals high in saturated fats should only be consumed in moderation.

Macadamia Nuts

While nuts are among the healthiest fats that may be consumed, not all nuts are created equal when following the ketogenic diet. Cashews, for instance, are abundant in carbs. Macadamia nuts are low in carbs and abundant in beneficial fat, making them a healthy fat source.

Virgin Coconut Oil

Saturated fat content is very high in virgin coconut oil. Using virgin coconut oil will guarantee that the oil contains a healthy proportion of naturally occurring plant compounds.

Tuna with Salmon

Whether you follow the ketogenic diet or not, there is no better way to get beneficial fats than by going out to sea."Omega-3 fatty acids, which are abundant in fatty fish and high in protein, have numerous health benefits for humans, including lowering inflammation and illness risk.

Pumpkin Seeds

"Seeds are rich in fatty acids (mono and polyunsaturated fatty acids) and provide a sufficient amount of protein" is another example of a healthy fat. In addition, seeds offer fiber, vitamins, minerals, and protein. Pumpkin seeds are a good choice because they are high in nutrients such as magnesium (an anti-inflammatory) and zinc (helpful for immunity).

Algae

Nutritionists and health-conscious keto dieters highly value algae as a food. Drinks high in fat can sustain ketosis.

Olive Oil

When following a ketogenic diet, getting your healthy fats from the proper source is crucial, so be sure you're getting the beneficial stuff. Olive-oil-rich diets have been shown to lower the risk of developing a number of illnesses. Use olive oil instead of butter when sautéing proteins and vegetables to help lower the amount of saturated fats that the body absorbs while eating a diet high in fat meals.

Avocados

Avocados are rich in antioxidants, fiber, and mono- and polyunsaturated fats, which are all considered health benefits. Avocados are a wonderful choice since they include fiber, which other fats—including oils—do not.

Eggs

Eggs are another essential component of keto cuisine. "A large egg provides 13 essential nutrients, 6 grams of high-quality proteins, 5 grams of total fat, and 1.5 grams of saturated fat.

Additionally, eggs are one of the many sources of vitamin D and contain choline, which is excellent for brain function, and antioxidants, which are best for eye problems."

Full-fat Coconut Milk

Full-fat coconut milk has a high fat content and contains MCTs (medium-chain triglycerides), which raise cholesterol and aid in energy production. It's particularly beneficial on smoothies and coffee.

Grass-fed Beef

You don't need to stock up on a ton of meat because a ketogenic diet is a high-fat diet as opposed to a high-protein diet. Steak has a lot of excellent protein and fat. Grass-fed steak provides a significant quantity of beneficial omega-3 fatty acids.

Exotic Oils

These consist of grape seed, walnut, avocado, and sesame oils. Plant-based exotic oils are monos and polys with low levels of saturated fats. They also have the same beneficial properties because they are derived from fatty foods high in antioxidants.

SHOPPING LIST WHEN ON A KETO DIST

The List

Knowing the ingredients you need would make creating your shopping list quite simple; so, this shopping list would be organized according to food types. On a book or paper, note it; on your phone, grab a screenshot of it; or memorize it. It saves time and is advisable to have a list you can always consult while shopping for your meals.

Vegetables

While on the ketogenic diet, veggies are a crucial component, so it is advisable to take them. However, avoid starchy kinds of vegetables, including potatoes. Not to worry; once you grow accustomed to the list above, you will be on roll.

Under vegetables we have: Broccoli; eggplant; Brussels sprouts; celery; kale; cabbage; mushrooms; arugula

Meat

On a ketogenic diet, meat is a very crucial component, so many people have advised meat as a good source of protein for ketogenic dieters.

Examples are Turkey; chicken; beef; lamb; pork; chicken

Dairy

Though it might be somewhat challenging to find dairy products fit for a ketogenic diet, some are still available. The dairy product you should buy should have the most calcium, protein, and fats—from grass-fed cows.

Feta cheese; crema cheese; cottage cheese; butter; Greek yogurt.

Fruits

Despite being warned against, you can still consume fruits in modest amounts. For those following a ketogenic diet, fruits offer several benefits, so fruit enthusiasts should not fear them since they can still enjoy them.

Tomatoes; lime; strawberries; lemon; coconut nuts and seeds; lime

Seeds & Nuts

Like any other diet, a healthy ketogenic one also includes seeds and nuts. Rich in protein and fat, they are ideal snack choices for whole-day consumption. Remember to always consider low-carb options.

Macadamia nuts; peecans; almonds; chia seeds; flaxseeds; cashews.

Seafood

For all ketogenic diets, seafood is excellent to have on your grocery list since it has protein and omega-3 fatty acids. Fresh is the finest way to get the taste you need while creating meals.

Salmon; cod; salmon; shrimp; mussels; tuna; egg.

Eggs

Eggs contain a lot of proteins. Make sure you buy the organic ones when shopping for them, make sure to buy organic ones. Always try to know the source and ensure you purchase organic eggs since there are eggs on the market made by birds given inferior boosters that could damage our bodies.

Oils

On the ketogenic diet, oils are excellent and healthy because they are very high in fats. Steer clear of oils heavy in trans fat.

Extra-virgin olive oil; avocado oil; nut oil; coconut oil

Keto-Friendly Snacks

Your neighborhood grocery shop has plenty of ketogenic snacks available.

- Dried seaweed
- Sugar-free beef jerky
- Low-carb variants

30 DAYS MEAL PLAN

Before you start your diet, make sure you have all the materials you need for the week. In the first week, we want to keep things basic. You take it slowly since you want the dietary changes to be mild on your mind and body. Your main focus should be on avoiding cravings, so attempt to gradually incorporate ketogenic foods into your meals. Start with a breakfast comprising lots of water, oats, fruits, quinoa, and eggs.

Try to sip lots of water at least two hours before breakfast. Furthermore, make sure you avoid drinking water for at least an hour after your meal. This should be strictly followed before and after every daily meal. The ketogenic diet functions as a natural diuretic, so you will often find yourself leaking. Not to worry; this is natural; just make sure your water and salt consumption stays high to balance electrolytes in the body. For best results, cut off dessert intake during the first two weeks. The dishes you could enjoy in your first week are shown below.

Week 1

	BREAKFAST	LUNCH	DINNER	DESSERTS
SUNDAY	Pancakes and Honey	Turkey Madeira	Lamb, cheese and cream Salad	Citrus Pudding
MONDAY	French Toast	Slow-cooked Ribs	Creamy Chicken Salad	Easy Caramel Rolls
TUESDAY	French Toast	Egg Salad	Chicken Chili	Crème Brule
WEDNESDAY	Pumpkin	Sweet	Autumn	Coconut

	Pancakes	and Sour Chicken	Vegetable Beef Stew	Cream Cookies
THURSDAY	French Toast	Thai Beef Stew	Kale and Onion Salad	Blueberry Cheesecake
FRIDAY	Chocolate Chip Waffles	Bacon and Italian Sausage Salad	Italian Zucchini Meatloaf	Caramel chocolate chip muffin
SATURDAY	Breakfast Quinoa	Tomato and Chicken salad	Lamb, cheese and cream Salad	Lemon Cheesecake

Week 2

Week one went so easily; we must keep week two as simple as possible. All you have to do the second week is stay on target. Start your morning with a cup of a cup of coffee. Starting your day with coffee shouldn't seem strange to you, as this coffee is infused with some butter, coconut oil, and whole cream. Here is a table with foods you could attempt in week two.

	BREAKFAST	LUNCH	DINNER	DESSERTS
SUNDAY	Pumpkin Pie Breakfast Sorghum	Chicken and Egg Salad	Cheesy Tortellini	Cream custard
MONDAY	Quinoa Breakfast Casserole	Stuffed Bell Peppers	Decadent Keto Meatloaf Recipe	Tiramisu
TUESD	Apple	Baco	Herb	Chocol

AY	Pie	n burritos	Baked Salmon	ate and Caramel Custard
WEDNESDAY	Zucchini Pancakes	Juicy Beef Salad	Hawaiian Pork	Blackberry muffin
THURSDAY	Apple Cherry Breakfast Risotto	Leftover Meatloaf	Meatloaf and Cheese	Strawberry Cheesecake
FRIDAY	Boiled Eggs with Toast	Vegetable Curry and Rice	Shrimp Marinara	Dark Chocolate Cake
SATURDAY	Tater Tot Egg Bake	Seafood Gumbo	Mixed Veggies with Rice	Coconut Rice Pudding

Week 3

Week 3 is now time for you to go faster with your diet plan; you have been able to stick to one for the first two weeks. In week three, we advise having breakfast at seven in the morning, lunch at one thirty-one, and dinner at seven thirty-nine. This will set aside six hours between every meal. The six-hour interval allows our body to break down excess fats faster.

	BREAKFAST	**LUNCH**	**DINNER**	**DESSERT**
SUNDAY	Korean Eggs	Chicken Taco Salad	Turkey and Pasta Primavera	Fruit and Nut Muffin
MONDAY	Breakfast Hash browns	Kingfish fillets	Lamb Curry and Rice	Chocolate Chip Cookies
TUESDAY	Apple-Oatme	Chicken	Beef Teriy	Pear and

	al	Teriyaki Salad	aki with Pineapple	Caramel Pudding
WEDNESDAY	Breakfast Pie	Chicken Tortillas	Turkey and Pasta Primavera	Classic Cheesecake
THURSDAY	Korean Eggs	Cheesy Tortellini	Beef and Onion Gravy with Noodles	Coconut Cream Macaroon
FRIDAY	Bread Pudding	Slow-Cooked Greens and Vegetables with Rice	Sesame Ginger Turkey Wraps	Caramel Fondue
SATURDAY	Crockpot sausag	Turkey Tetra	Pork & Mushr	Chocolate Brown

	e cheddar casserole	zzini	ooms	ies

Week 4

We are going to try all conceivable ways to miss breakfast and lunch since we are going to be drinking lots of water in week 4, the last week of our diet. You are free to take as much coffee, water, and tea as you like. In place of refined sugar, use honey in beverages. Dinners will be fantastic; you can also have ketogenic desserts. Week four will be quite easy to follow the food plan, as your body is now adjusting to it.

	BREAKFAST	**LUNCH**	**DINNER**	**DESSERTS**
SUNDAY	Onion and	Parmesan	Cajun	Unbaked

	Kale Frittata	Risotto	Shrimp and Rice	Chocolate Cake
MONDAY	Cream Cheese Omelet	Chicken bake	Plum pork Tenderloin	Cheddar Pepper Biscuits
TUESDAY	Omelet with Feta and Spinach	Korean Beef	Herbed Chicken with Olives	Dark chocolate Cupcakes
WEDNESDAY	Goat Cheese and Zucchini Frittata	Baked Carp	Greek Salad with a Lemon and Vinegar Dressing	Cinnamon and coffee Cookies

THURSDAY	Spinach and Mushroom Quiche	Chicken Guadalajara	Vegan Chili	Big Philly Cheesecake
FRIDAY	Broiled Spanish Mackerel	Enchilada Orzo	Fisherman Stew	Coffee muffin
SATURDAY	Tomato and Basil Sandwiches	Vegetarian Buffalo Cauliflower Chili	Toasted Herb Rice	Strawberry Brownies

Week 5

Try these in the last two days of the diet.

	BREAKFAST	LUNCH	DINNER	DESSERTS
DAY	Bacon and Eggs	Mediterranean Style	Red Beans	Coffee Cake

1		Halibut	with Rice	
DAY 2	Strawberry and Roasted Oats	Vegetable burritos	Cheese and onion Quiche	Chocolate Cheesecake

BREAKFAST RECIPES
Chocoholic granola

Serves: 14

Prep time: 5 minutes, plus 20 minutes to cool

Cook time: 10 minutes

Ingredients:

- 2 tablespoons of water
- ½ cup (65g) Erythritol
- 1 teaspoon of ground cinnamon
- 1 teaspoon vanilla extract
- ¾ teaspoon very finely ground sea salt
- 27 g, or ¼ cup, cocoa powder
- 3 cups (190 g) of unsweetened coconut flakes

instructions:

1. Leave aside a parchment-paper-sealed baking sheet.

2. If you are using confectioners'-style erythritol, move to Step 3; if using granulated erythritol, leave it to simmer

until you can no longer feel the grains under the spoon. Place the vanilla, erythritol, and water in a large fry pan on medium-low heat. Leave it to simmer lightly, and stir every 30 seconds.

3. Low the heat; then add the cinnamon, cocoa powder, and salt; gently stir until the salt, cocoa powder, and cinnamon stick are well combined.

4. Cook for approximately 6 to 7 minutes until the bottom portion of the pan starts to stick. Combine the coconut flakes and keep them constantly swirling at a low temperature to avoid burning.

5. Either move to a 1-quart (950-ml) or large covered container for storing, or get it off from the heat and place the granola on parchment paper and allow it to totally cool for about 20 minutes before you eat it.

Nutritional Information:

Calories: 106

Fat: 78%

Carbs: 19%

Protein: 3%

Herb Chicken Sausages With Braised Bok Choy

Serves 5

Prep time: 5 minutes

Cook time: 25 minutes

Ingredients:

Chicken sausages:

- ¾ teaspoon finely ground sea salt
- 1 minced clove of garlic
- 1 pound (455 grams) of ground chicken
- 5 cups of 350 grams sliced bok choy
- ½ tsp. fresh thyme leaves
- 1 tablespoon of freshly chopped chives
- 2 teaspoons chopped white onions
- ⅛ teaspoon red pepper flakes
- 2 freshly cut sage leaves.

- 1 teaspoon chopped fresh parsley
- ½ teaspoon ground black pepper
- 3 tablespoons coconut oil, avocado oil, or ghee for the pan

Instructions:

1. In a large mixing bowl, toss all the ingredients intended for the sausages until they are well blended.

2. In a large saucepan set on ordinary (medium-low) heat, broil the oil.

3. Using a ¼-cup (60-ml) scoop, scoop up and shape the chicken mixture using your hands to create ten balls roughly 1¾(4.5 cm) in diameter. Place the balls in the heated saucepan and compress until the patties are approximately 6 mm thick.

4. Leave the sausages cooking for around ten minutes on each side, or until they turn well cooked and golden on the outside.

5. Arrange the sausages on a serving plate; to warm them, bake them at 180°F (82°C).

6. Put the bok choy in the identical pan, seal, and cook for roughly five minutes at medium heat, or until it gets soft.

7. Arrange the cooked bok choi alongside the sausages on the serving plate.

Nutritional Information:

Calories: 246

Fat: 52%

Carbs: 4%

Protein: 44%

Avocado Breakfast Muffins
Makes 12 muffins (2 per serving)

Prep time: 5 minutes

Cook time: 25 minutes

Ingredients:

- 8 big eggs

- Pinch some finely ground sea salt.
- ½ cup (120 ml) pure-fat coconut milk
- 1½ tablespoons powdered garlic
- Ground black pepper's pinch
- ¼ cup (20 grams) freshly chopped fresh cilantro leaves and stems.
- 1½ tsp. onion powder
- 3 tablespoons of nutritional yeast
- 1 finely chopped, seeded jalapeño pepper
- Peel, pit, and cube 1 medium Hass avocado (approximately 4 ounces or 110 g of flesh).

Instructions:

1. Either use a silicone muffin pan without liners or stuff, a well-sized 12 muffin pan, using muffin liners, at about 350°F.

2. Transfer the entire contents into a medium-sized mixing basin and stir until completely combined.

3. Bake until the muffin becomes clean when you put a toothpick into the middle for 23 to 25 minutes. Evenly split

the batter between the packed muffin wells and fill each to approximately 3¼ full.

4. Present and savor.

Nutritional Information:

Calories: 160

FAT: 63%

CARBS: 11%

PROTEIN: 26%

Buffalo chicken breakfast muffins
Makes 12 muffins (2 per serving)

Prep time: 5 minutes

Cook time: 20 minutes

Ingredients:

- 8 large eggs.
- 2 teaspoons of garlic powder
- A pinch of ground black pepper
- 1 cup (185 grams) of shredded cooked chicken
- 4 finely chopped green onions
- A handful of very fine sea salt

- ¼ cup plus two tablespoons (80 g) of coconut oil or ghee
- 1 teaspoon of spicy sauce

Instructions:

1. Preheat your oven to 350°F (177°C), then line a well sized muffin pan with muffin liners or a silicone muffin pan without liners.

2. Transfer all the ingredients into a well-sized mixing bowl and stir until completely combined.

3. Evenly split the batter between the lined muffin wells, filling each to roughly 3¼ full. Bake for 18 to 20 minutes, or until the muffins pull out clean when a toothpick is inserted in the middle.

Nutritional Information:

Calories: 269

Carbs: 3%

Fat: 71%

Protein: 26%

Prosciutto biscuits

Makes 12 biscuits (2 per serving)

Prep time: 10 minutes

Cook time: 20 minutes

Ingredients:

- 6 large eggs.
- ½ teaspoonful baking powder
- ¾ cup (155g) mayonnaise
- 3 Sliced green onions coarsely, focusing only on the green parts.
- 1 cup (100 g) of coconut flour
- 12 finely chopped slices of prosciutto, around 3½ ounces/100 g

Instructions:

1. Preheat the oven to 375°F (190°C). Stow a baking sheet, either with parchment paper or a silicone baking mat.

2. Pour the eggs and mayonnaise into a mixing basin, then whisk to combine.

3. Stir in the green onions and chopped prosciutto. Combine the mayonnaise mixture with the dry ingredients and stir well to blend completely. Place the baking powder and coconut flour in a medium-sized mixing bowl and mix well.

4. Repeat the process for the remaining dough pieces, which are evenly split into 12 portions. After separating the dough into balls on your palms, place it on the lined baking sheet and compress with your palm until it gets thick to roughly an inch (2.5 cm).

5. Bake for roughly 15 to 20 minutes until the sides and edges of the biscuits begin to turn golden.

6. Get it out of the oven and enjoy.

Nutritional Information:

Calories: 299

Fat: 82%

Carbs: 4%

Protein: 14%

Salmon bacon rolls with dipping sauce

Makes 16 rolls (4 per serving)

Prep time: 10 minutes

Cook time: 10 minutes

Ingredients:

- 8 ounces (225 g) of smoked salmon Cut into 16 squares.
- 8 slices of bacon (about eight ounces or 225 grams).

Dipping Source:

- 2 teaspoons of sugar-free barbecue sauce
- Mayonnaise cup (105 g)

Instructions:

1. For about 8 to 10 minutes, cook the bacon in a heavy skillet on medium heat until a lot of the fat is gone and the bacon is brown but not crispy.

2. Put a square of salmon on the edge of a bacon strip. Pin around the salmon in the bacon and keep firm using a

toothpick, then place on a plate. Repeat the same process for the for the bacon and salmon that are left, giving a total of 16 rolls.

3. After mixing, serve the barbecue sauce and mayonnaise with the salmon rolls in a medium-sized bowl.

Nutritional Information:

Calories: 324

Fat: 79%

Carbs: 4%

Protein: 17%

Pumpkin spice latte overnight "oats."

Serves: 2

Prep time: 5 minutes, plus 8 hours to soak (not including time to brew coffee)

Cook time: —

Ingredients:

- ½ teaspoon ground nutmeg
- Half a teaspoon of vanilla essence
- ¼ teaspoon of Ground cloves
- ½ cup (75 g) hulled hemp seeds
- Pinch of finely ground sea salt
- ⅓ cup (80 ml) Made decaf or regular brewed coffee
- ¼ teaspoon ground cinnamon
- 2 teaspoons of pureed canned pumpkin
- 1 tablespoon of chia seeds.
- 2 tablespoons of erthritol or three drops of liquid stevia
- ½ cup (80 ml) milk (normal or non-dairy)

TOPPINGS (optional):

- Ground cinnamon
- Extra hemp seeds with hullings
- Raw or roasted pecans, chopped
- Toasted, shredded coconut, free from sugar

Instructions:

1. Seal it and place it in the refrigerator to marinate overnight or for 8 hours. Set all the ingredients in a 12-ounce (350-ml) bowl with a cover and whisk until they mix well.

2. Split into two bowls, add more milk until it tastes as desired, top as you like, and enjoy.

Nutritional Information:

Calories: 337

Fat: 71%

Carbs: 11%

Protein: 18%

Keto Coffee Recipe

Makes one 12-ounce (350-ml) serving

Prep time: 1 minute (not including time to brew coffee)

Cook time: —

Ingredients:

- ¼ teaspoon vanilla extract

- Two teaspoons of full-fat coconut milk
- 0.1 ounce (3 grams) of optional cordyceps
- ½ teaspoon endogenous ketones
- 1¼ cups (300 ml) of hot brewed coffee (normal or decaf).
- Tablespoon collagen peptides or protein powder
- Tablespoon coconut oil, unflavored MCT powder, or ghee
- drops of liquid stevia or one teaspoon of erythritol

Instructions:

1. Put all the ingredients in a blender and blend for twenty to thirty seconds, until they are well blended. Another alternative is for you to put all the ingredients in a covered bottle made of stainless steel or Thermos and then shake for roughly ten seconds.

2. Move to a large coffee mug and present it right away.

Nutritional Information:

Calories: 334

Fat: 78%

Carbs: 0%

Protein: 22%

Rocket fuel hot chocolate

MAKES two 10-ounce (300-ml) servings

Prep time: 5 minutes

Cook time: —

Ingredients:

- 1 teaspoon of coconut butter
- Ground cinnamon pinch (optional)
- 2 tablespoons of cocoa powder
- 2 teaspoons of powdered collagen peptides or protein
- 2 cups (475 ml) of heated milk—regular or nonfat
- 2 tablespoons coconut oil; MCT oil; unflavored MCT oil powder; ghee
- 1 tablespoon of e-erythritol or four drops of liquid stevia

Instructions:

1. Put all the ingredients in a blender and run for roughly ten seconds, or until they are well mixed.

2. Divide into two mugs; if you want, sprinkle cinnamon and enjoy!

Nutritional Information:

Calories: 357

Fat: 74%

Carbs: 12%

Protein: 14%

Cross-country scrambler

Serves 2

Prep time: 5 minutes

Cook time: 28 minutes

Ingredients:

- 6 big, well-beaten eggs
- 8 slices of bacon (about eight ounces or 225 grams).
- ½ teaspoon ground black pepper

- ½ sliced green bell pepper
- packed cup of spiral-sliced butternut squash (approximately 5¼ oz/150 g).
- ½ cup (40 g) chopped green onions—green parts alone

Instructions:

1. Cook the bacon in a large saucepan on medium heat for about 15 minutes until it gets crispy. Take the bacon out of the pan with the grease in the pan. When the bacon is cool, crumble it.

2. Add the bell pepper and squash to the bacon grease pan, seal it, and simmer on medium-low heat for 8 minutes until the vegetables soften.

3. Add the black pepper, green onions, and beaten eggs; mix well with a large spoon.

4. Wrap in half of the crumbled bacon once you're done. Uncover it and cook for five minutes, stirring each minute until the eggs cook to your liking.

5. Evenly distribute two dishes, top with the remaining crumbled bacon, and savor!

Nutritional Information:

Calories: 395

Fat: 62%

Carbs: 12%

Protein: 26%

Full meal deal

Serves 4

Prep time: 10 minutes (this doesn't include time to make biscuits or chimichurri)

Cook time: 3 minutes

Ingredients:

- ✓ 2 mug biscuits (here).
- ✓ ½ cup (105 g) chimichurri (here)
- ✓ 2 cups (140 g) of fresh spinach
- ✓ 1 tablespoon of avocado oil

- ✓ 1 big Hass avocado, peeled, pitted, and mashed—about six ounces or 170 grams of flesh.

Instructions:

1. Halve the biscuits, then arrange each half on a separate dish. Top each half with the mashed avocado in equal measure.

2. Put the oil in a medium-sized frying pan set on normal heat; sauté the spinach for roughly three minutes until it wilts somewhat.

3. Top the avocado with the wilted spinach; then, add two tablespoons of chimichurri to every plate and enjoy.

Nutritional Information:

Calories: 358

Fat: 85%

Protein: 8%

Carbs: 7%

Liver sausages & onions

Serves 6

Prep time: 10 minutes, plus 24 hours to soak livers

Cook time: 26 minutes

Ingredients:

Sausages:

- 4 minced cloves of garlic
- 8 ounces (225 g) of chicken livers
- ½ tablespoons dried sage, rubbed coarsely
- tablespoon apple cider vinegar
- 1 teaspoon of dried thyme leaves
- 1 pound (455 g) of ground beef
- ¾ teaspoon ground black pepper
- 1 pound (455 grams) of ground pork
- 1¼ teaspoon dried rosemary leaves
- 1 teaspoon of coarsely crushed sea salt
- moderately large white onions, thinly sliced

- ¼ cup (55 g) coconut oil or ghee or ¼ cup (60 ml) avocado oil, for the pan.

Instructions:

1. Put the chicken livers in a medium-sized basin, fill with water, add vinegar, seal, and store in the refrigerator to marinate for roughly one to two days.

2. After clearing fluids from the livers, mix until they become smooth.

3. Move the liquefied livers to a large mixing bowl and add the left-over sausage ingredients, using your hands to properly incorporate them.

4. Over medium-low heat, cook the oil in a large pot.

5. Making use of a ¼-cup scoop, scoop up portions of the mixture and spin in between your hands to make 12 balls that are roughly 1¾" in diameter as the oil heats. Place the balls on the heated pan and compress until they are ½ "which is about 1.25 cm thick." Steer clear of crowding the pan; instead,

create the sausages at varying intervals so they can comfortably fit in should they not be able to control themselves.

6. Cook the sauces' sides for eight minutes, until the pink in the middle goes off.

7. Arrange the cooked sausages on a serving tray. To make the oven warm—if you so want—set it to 180°F (82°C).

8. When the sausages are cooked, put the sliced onions in the same skillet and, with constant stirring every minute, cook for roughly ten minutes until they become translucent.

9. Arrange the sautéed onions on the sausage plate and enjoy.

Nutritional information:

Calories: 392

Fat: 50%

Carbs: 6%

Protein: 43.2%

Eggs benedict

Serves 4

Prep time: 10 minutes (not including time to make biscuits or hollandaise)

Cook time: 16 minutes

Ingredients:

- 4 large eggs
- Muesli biscuits
- 4 slices of Canadian bacon
- teaspoons of apple cider vinegar
- tablespoons freshly chopped fresh parsley For garnishing.
- ½ cup (120 ml) Hollandaise Sauce is ready in seconds here.

Instructions:

1. Halve the biscuits and arrange each half on separate plates.

2. Fill a large saucepan with water up to two-thirds, and allow to boil for some minutes, once it starts to simmer, add

the vinegar once it reaches an average (medium-low) heat level.

3. Break each egg into separate dishes, one for each egg, and then add the eggs to the lightly simmering water. Once the egg begins to turn white, add one more egg, and continue to add the eggs one by one until the saucepan is full. Cook for about two minutes, then remove from the heat and let the eggs sit in boiling water for 8 minutes before removing with a slotted spoon.

4. Place the Canadian bacon in a large fry pan and fry for three minutes on each side over medium heat until brown.

5. Top each half of the biscuits with a poached egg and a piece of Canadian bacon; then, finish each half with hollandaise sauce, 2 tbsp.

6. Drizzle with parsley and enjoy.

Nutritional information:

Calories: 399

Fat: 86%

Carbs: 6%

Protein: 8%

Pepper sausage fry

Serves: 4

Prep time: 5 minutes

Cook time: 20 minutes

Ingredients:

- teaspoon of paprika
- ¼ cup (55 grams) coconut oil, or ¼ cup (60 ml) avocado oil
- ½ teaspoon garlic powder
- Slice 12 ounces (340 g) of smoked sausages thinly.
- ½ teaspoon coarsely ground sea salt
- thinly sliced, tiny green bell pepper
- 1 teaspoon of dry oregano leaves
- 1 thinly sliced, tiny red bell pepper
- ½ cup (17 grams) chopped fresh parsley
- ½ teaspoon ground black pepper

Instructions:

1. In a large saucepan set on an ordinary (medium-low) heat, warm the oil until it begins to shimmer.

2. Add the other ingredients as soon as the oil starts to shimmer, but the parsley is not necessary. Seal, then cook for about fifteen minutes, until the bell peppers are soft.

3. Remove the lid and keep cooking until the liquid evaporates for roughly five to six minutes.

4. Remove from the fire, stir in the parsley, and serve.

Nutritional information:

Calories: 411

Fat: 84%

Carbs: 6%

Protein: 10%

Keto breakfast pudding

Serves 3

Prep time: 5 minutes

Cook time: —

Ingredients:

- teaspoon of vanilla extract
- 350 ml, 1 ½ cups full-fat coconut milk
- tablespoon of apple cider vinegar
- 1 cup (110 grams) of frozen raspberries
- teaspoons of chia seeds
- ¼ cup (40 g) unflavored MCT oil powder; ¼ cup (60 ml) MCT oil or melted coconut oil
- 1 tablespoon e-erythritol, four drops liquid stevia
- ¼ cup (40 g) collagen peptides or protein powder

TOPPINGS (Optional)

- Unsweetened, shredded coconut
- Selected fresh berries of preference
- Hemp seeds that have been hulled

Instructions:

1. Blend all the components and run till they become smooth.

2. Present it in bowl, styled with toppings.

Nutritional Information:

Calories: 403

Fat: 76%

Protein: 15%

Carbs: 9%

Something different breakfast Sammy

Serves 1

Prep time: 5 minutes

Cook time: 10 minutes

Ingredients:

- 1 medium Hass avocado, peeled and pitted—roughly 4 ounces or 110 grams of flesh.
- 1 teaspoon of mayonnaise
- 1 half-ripped lettuce leaf
- 1 red onion ring.

- Pinch the ground black pepper.
- slice of tomato
- Cook two strips of bacon—roughly two ounces or 55 grams—until crispy.
- Pinch of coarsely crushed sea salt
- Pinch the optional poppy or sesame seeds.

Instructions:

1. Cook the bacon in a medium-sized frying pan set on average (middle) heat until it crisps, for about ten minutes.

2. On a plate, arrange half of the cut avocado.

3. Arrange the lettuce bits over the top of each avocado half; then, on the lettuce, spread the mayonnaise; top the lettuce with tomato, onion, and bacon; subsequently, sprinkle with the pepper and salt.

4. If using seeds, seal the stack with the other half of the split avocado and sprinkle; then, serve and enjoy!

Nutritional Information:

Calories: 545

Fat: 72%

Carbs: 14%

Protein: 14%

Mug biscuit

Serves 1

Prep time: 1 minute

Cook time: 2 minutes

Ingredients:

- 1 large egg.
- ½ tsp baking powder
- 28 grams (¼ cup) of blanched almond flour
- teaspoon apple cider vinegar
- 1 tablespoon coconut flour
- ¼ teaspoon coarsely ground sea salt
- 1 tablespoon softened coconut oil or ghee + extra for serving if preferred.

Instructions:

1. Pour all the ingredients into a cup with a minimum of 2" (5 cm) in diameter. Mix until they are fully blended; then, use a spoon to level them.

2. Place the mug in the microwave and let it cook for 1.5 minutes.

3. Remove the mug from the microwave and insert a clean toothpick. If batter remains on the toothpick, microwave the biscuit for an additional 15 to 30 seconds until clean.

4. While the biscuit is still warm, slather it with the fat you desire. Place the mug on a clean plate and move it gently until the biscuit frees the mug.

Nutritional information:

Calories: 399

Fat: 76%

Carbs: 10%

Protein: 14%

All day any day hash

Serves 4

Prep time: 10 minutes

Cook time: 25 minutes

Ingredients:

- 55 g i.e ¼ cup coconut oil or ghee
- teaspoon of fresh thyme leaves
- ⅔ cup (one hundred grams) of sliced white onions
- ½ teaspoon coarsely ground sea salt
- garlic cloves, minced
- 25 g, or ¼ cup, crushed pork rinds
- medium turnips (approximately 1 lb/455 g), Peeled and diced
- 1 slice of red bell pepper
- 2 medium carrots, roughly five ounces or 140 grams, chopped
- ½ cup (120 ml) creamy Italian dressing
- ⅛ teaspoon ground black pepper
- 2 freshly chopped parsley leaves
- 8 ounces (225 g) of Thinly sliced boneless steak weighing

Instructions:

1. Place and heat the oil inside a large frying pan over ordinary (middle) heat, then add the garlic and onions. Cook for five to seven minutes until transparent.

2. Add the steak, turnips, bell peppers, and carrots; toss to coat; seal, and then cook for 15 to 18 minutes, ensuring you stir at three-minute intervals until the turnips grow tender and the steak cooks nicely to your taste. Take the pan off the heat.

3. Add the smashed pig rinds, pepper, parsley, salt, and thyme, then toss it to coat.

4. Evenly distribute the hash among four medium-sized dishes and top each with two tablespoons of dressing before you serve.

Nutritional Information:

Calories: 512

Fat: 66%

Protein: 21%

Carbs: 13%

Indian masala omelet

Makes 1 large omelet (2 servings)

Prep time: 8 minutes

Cook time: 25 minutes

Ingredients:

- 6 large, beaten eggs.
- 3 tablespoons of either ghee, coconut oil, or avocado oil.
- A small, chopped tomato
- ¼ cup (20 grams) chopped green onions
- ½ teaspoon garam masala
- 1 minced clove of garlic
- 1½ teaspoon curry powder
- 1 green chili pepper, finely chopped and seeded.
- ¼ cup (15 grams) chopped fresh cilantro leaves and stems.

Instructions:

1. Put the oil into a large frying pan and heat on medium heat, as the oil shimmers, add the chili pepper, green onions, tomato, and garlic. Cook to evaporate the liquid from the tomatoes for 10 minutes on a large fry pan set on medium heat.

2. Lower the heat, then sprinkle the tomato mixture with garam masala and curry powder; stir to incorporate; then top with beaten eggs.

3. Carefully seal and cook the edges for five minutes.

4. Drizzle with the cilantro, fold one side to the other, seal the lid, and simmer for an additional ten minutes.

5. Get it off the stove, chop it in two, and present it.

Nutritional Information:

Calories: 438

Fat: 75%

Carbs: 7%

Protein: 18%

Sticky wrapped eggs

Makes 12 wrapped eggs (2 per serving)

Prep time: 10 minutes (not including time to hard-boil eggs)

Cook time: 30 minutes

Ingredients:

- 12 hard-boiled eggs;
- ¼ cup (60 ml) coconut aminos;
- 2 tablespoons spicy sauce;
- 12 slices bacon, around 12 ounces/340 g
- 6 cups (100 g) arugula;

Instructions:

1. Turn the oven's temperature to 400°F (205°C.). Arrange a 12-well standard-sized muffin pan with muffin liners; alternatively, use a silicone muffin pan, which does not require liners.

2. Put the coconut aminos and hot sauce in a bowl and whisk to thoroughly

mix. Arrange the basin next to the muffin pan.

3. Break the boiling eggs. After wrapping each egg and bacon strip one after the other, soak it in the hot sauce mixture and then carefully place it inside a muffin pan.

4. Bake for almost half an hour, then flip the eggs over midway.

5. Divide the arugula equally among six little serving dishes. As toppings, add two sticky eggs and sauces from muffin liners.

Nutritional Information:

Calories: 438

Fat: 67%

Carbs: 3%

Protein: 30%

Coffee shake

Makes one 14-ounce (415-ml) serving

Prep time: 5 minutes

Cook time: —

Ingredients:

- 1cup (240 ml) full-fat coconut milk
- 4 ice cubes
- 4 ice cubes; 1 ½ tbsp. cocoa powder
- ½ cup (120 ml) water
- ½ teaspoon instant coffee granules
- tablespoons unflavored MCT oil powder or ghee
- 1 ½ teaspoons erythritol or 2 drops liquid stevia

Instructions:

1. Put all the ingredients in a blender and run them until the ice breaks down entirely and the shake's texture smooths.

2. Change to a big glass and present it right away.

Nutritional Information:

Calories: 757

Fat:91%

Carbs:6%

Protein: 3%

Super breakfast combo

Serves 1

Prep time: 10 minutes

Cook time: —

Ingredients:

CHOCOLATE FAT BOMBS:

- teaspoon of cocoa powder
- tablespoon coconut butter
- teaspoons coconut oil;
- ½ teaspoon confectioners'-style erythritol; or one drop liquid stevia

MATCHA LATTE:

- tablespoons collagen peptides or protein powder
- cup (240 ml) boiling water
- 1 teaspoon erythritol or two drops liquid stevia
- 1 teaspoon matcha powder.
- 1¼ cups (300 ml) heated, full-fat coconut milk

- 1 tablespoon nut butter, coconut butter, or coconut oil
- ½ teaspoon maca powder (optional)
- ¼ teaspoon chaga powder; or ashwagandha powder(optional)

Instructions:

1. Put all the components in a bowl when making the fat bomb; you can either place it in the microwave for roughly twenty to thirty seconds or let it dissolve under the sun. Anyone is cool as soon as the coconut butter melts; properly whisk and transport to a paper muffin liner, a silicone mold formed of plastic container. To cause it to become firm, freeze it for five minutes.

2. For now, place the boiling water, matcha, collagen, sweetener, coconut butter, maca, and chaga, if you are using it in a 20-ounce or large mug. Whisk thoroughly until the components combine correctly; the lumps vanish after around one minute. Stir while adding the hot coconut milk.

3. Dish the latte and the cold fat.

Nutritional Information:

Calories: 740

Fat: 80%

Carbs: 6%

Protein: 14%

Delicious Coconut Flour Waffles
Serves: 5

Ingredients:

- 4 tbsp. coconut flour
- 5 eggs, separated by white and yolk
- tsp. baking powder
- 4-5 tbsp. granulated stevia or your own sweetener
- tbsp. whole milk
- 1 tsp. vanilla
- 4½ oz. butter, melted

Instructions:

1. In a bowl, whisk the egg whites until stiff peaks form.

2. Combine the egg yolk, baking powder, stevia or other sweetener, and coconut flour in a separate bowl.

3. Melt the butter and add it. Mix the batter gradually until it becomes smooth.

4. Stir in the vanilla and milk.

5. Mix the contents from the two bowls together, folding the mixture to maintain the batter's fluff.

6. Once the waffle maker has warmed up, pour some of the waffle mixture into it. It's done when it turns golden brown. Continue until the batter is all used.

Nutritional Information:

Calories: 277

Fat: 22g

Protein: 8g

Net carbs: 4.3g

Keto Cream Cheese Pancakes

Serves: 8 to 10

Ingredients:

- 4 eggs
- tbsp. sugar substitute
- 4 oz. cream cheese, softened
- 4 tbsp. coconut flour
- Almond milk as needed
- 1½ tsp. baking powder
- tsp. vanilla extract

Instructions:

1. Using a blender or mixer, combine the cream cheese, sugar replacement, eggs and vanilla.

2. Mix in the baking powder and coconut flour. Mix thoroughly. After a few minutes, if the batter gets thick, thin it out with a little almond milk.

3. Preheat the 325°F electric griddle. Shape the batter into 5-inch rounds.

4. When the surface begins to bubble, turn it over. Cook for a further 2 to 4 minutes, or until browned.

5. It can be used for sandwiches or served with your preferred toppings.

Nutritional Information:

Calories: 100

Fat: 8g

Net Carb: 3.5g

Protein: 5g

Yummy Avocado And Salmon Breakfast Boats

Serves: 1

Ingredients:

- 1 avocado
- 2 oz. smoked salmon
- 1 oz. fresh goat cheese
- 2 tbsp. of organic extra virgin olive oil
- 2 tbsp. lemon juice
- A dash of sea salt

Instructions:

1. Halve the avocado and take out the stone.

2. Place the remaining ingredients inside the avocado after processing the salmon, goat cheese, oil, lemon juice, and salt in a food processor until the mixture is creamy.

3. Have fun!

Nutritional Information:

Calories: 520

Net Carbs: 5g

Fat: 45g

Protein: 20g

Healthy Vegetable Breakfast Hash
Serves: 1

Ingredients:

- 1 medium zucchini
- 2 oz. bacon
- ¼ cup white onion

- 1 tbsp. coconut oil Fresh parsley, chopped
- Salt to taste
- 1 large egg

Instructions:

1. Chop the onion and zucchini, and slice the bacon.

2. Add the bacon after you've sautéed the onion over medium heat. Cook, stirring, until just beginning to brown.

3. Cook the zucchini for 10 to 15 minutes after adding it to the pan.

4. After it's finished, put the hash on a platter and sprinkle with the parsley.

5. Add a fried egg or, if you're not eating eggs, avocado on top.

Nutritional Information:

Calories: 427

Net Carbs: 7g

Fat: 35g

Protein: 17g

Sausage Casserole with Vegetables

Serves: 6

Ingredients:

- 2 cups zucchini, diced
- 3 eggs
- ¼ cup onion, diced
- 1 tbsp. dried ground sage
- cups cabbage, shredded
- 2 tbsp. mustard
- 1 lb. pork sausage
- Cayenne pepper
- ½ cup mayonnaise
- 1½ cups cheddar cheese, shredded

Instructions:

1. Set the oven temperature to 375°F. Grease and reserve a casserole dish.

3. Cook the sausage and the vegetables in a big skillet over medium heat until they are soft.

4. Fill the casserole dish with the mixture.

5. Whisk together the eggs, mayonnaise, mustard, sage, and pepper in a separate bowl.

6. Stir the egg mixture for one minute after adding the shredded cheese.

7. Turn the mixture onto the sausage and veggies in the casserole dish, then sprinkle the cheese on top.

8. Bake for 30 minutes, or until the cheese is melted on top and the casserole is bubbling around the edges.

Nutritional Information:

Calories: 480

Net Carbs: 5g

Protein: 20g

Fat: 42g

Breakfast Tacos

Serves: 3.

Ingredients:

- 1 cup mozzarella cheese, shredded
- Salt and pepper
- 2 tbsp. butter
- 3 strips of bacon
- 6 eggs

- ½ an avocado
- 1 oz. cheddar cheese, shredded

Instructions:

1. Cook for 12 to 15 minutes, or until the bacon is crispy, at 375°F on an aluminum foil-covered baking pan.

2. In the meantime, coat the bottom of a nonstick skillet with a third of the mozzarella. On medium heat, cook for two to three minutes, or until the edges start to brown.

3. Remove the mozzarella from the pan (it will now resemble a taco shell) using a pair of tongs. Continue with the leftover cheese.

4. Eggs should be scrambled, Season to taste with salt and pepper, and stir frequently. stir often.

5. Place the eggs, avocado, and bacon inside the shells. Top with a sprinkle of cheddar cheese. Add cilantro or spicy sauce (optional).

Nutritional Information:

Calories: 440

Net Carbs: 4g

Fat: 36g

Protein: 26g

Keto Lemon Muffins With Poppy Seeds

Serves: 12

Ingredients:

- 3/4 cup almond flour
- 1 tbsp. baking powder
- ⅓ cup Erythritol
- ¼ cup Flaxseed meal
- ¼ cup Butter, melted 3 eggs
- Lemon zest of 2 lemons
- 2 tbsp. poppy seeds
- ¼ cup Heavy cream
- 3 tbsp. lemon juice
- 20 drops liquid sweetener
- 1 tbsp. vanilla

Instructions:

1. Set the oven temperature to 345°F.

2. In the meantime, combine the erythritol, poppy seeds, almond flour, and flaxseed meal in a bowl.

3. When the mixture is smooth, add the melted butter and stir in the heavy cream and eggs. Mix in the remaining ingredients.

4. After dividing the splitting into 12 cups, pour the batter into the muffin pan and bake for 18 to 20 minutes.

5. Take it out of the oven and allow it cool for about ten minutes.

Nutritional Information:

Calories: 130

Net Carbs: 1.7g

Fat: 11.5g

Protein: 4g

Cheddar And Bacon Omelets With Chives

Serves: 1

Ingredients:

- 2 slices of bacon
- 2 eggs
- 2 tbsp. bacon grease
- 2 stalks of chives
- Salt and pepper
- 1 oz. cheddar cheese

Instructions:

1. Melt the bacon grease in a pan that has been preheated to medium-low heat. Add the salt, pepper, chives, and eggs. Gently stir.

2. When the edges are set, add the bacon. Cook for an additional 20–30 seconds.

3. Fold the omelet in half after adding the cheese. Turn over and allow the other side to warm through.

Nutritional Information:

Calories: 460

Net Carbs: 2g

Fat: 40g

Protein: 25g

Salted Caramel Cereal With Pork Rinds

Serves: 1

Ingredients:

- 2 tbsp. butter
- 1 oz. pork rinds
- 1 cup vanilla coconut milk
- ¼ tbsp. ground cinnamon
- 2 tbsp. heavy cream
- 1 tbsp. erythritol

Instructions:

1. Add the butter to a pan over medium heat and whisk until golden.

2. Take it out and stir in the erythritol and heavy cream. Stir thoroughly and put it back on the burner. Stir continuously and keep heating until the mixture reaches the desired caramel color.

3. Make sure the pork rinds are equally coated by adding and mixing them in.

4. Place them in a jar and refrigerate for 20 to 45 minutes for them to cool down.

Nutritional Information:

Calories: 510

Net Carbs: 2.7g

Fat: 50g

Protein: 15g

Pumpkin Bread

Serves: 10

Ingredients:

- 1½ cups almond flour
- ¼ cup granulated sugar
- 3 egg whites
- ¼ cup psyllium husk powder
- ½ cup coconut milk
- 1½ tsp. pumpkin pie spice
- ½ tsp. salt
- 2 tsp. baking powder

Instructions:

1. Sift all of the dry ingredients into a bowl. Put a jar containing one cup of water in a preheated 350°F oven.

2. Combine the dry ingredients with the pumpkin and coconut milk, mixing thoroughly.

3. After whisking the egg whites, carefully incorporate them into the dough.

4. After putting the dough in a loaf pan that has been oiled, bake the bread for 75 minutes.

Nutritional Information:

Calories: 120

Net Carbs: 3g

Fat: 9g

Protein: 5g

Red Chocolate Doughnuts

Serves: 9.

Ingredients:

For the doughnut:

- 1 tsp. red food coloring
- ¼ cup Erythritol
- 2 tbsp. cocoa powder
- ½ cup coconut flour
- ½ cup coconut milk
- ½ tbsp. vanilla extract
- ¼ cup coconut oil
- ¼ tsp. salt
- ¼ tsp. apple cider vinegar
- ¼ tsp. baking soda 4 eggs
- ¼ tsp. liquid stevia

For the iting:

- ¼ cup powdered erythritol
- 4 tbsp. butter
- 4 oz. cream cheese
- ½ tsp. vanilla extract
- tbsp. heavy cream
- tsp. red food coloring

Instructions:

1. Mix the baking soda, cocoa powder, salt, and coconut flour after sieving them.

2. Stir in the eggs, erythritol, milk, vanilla, and red food with the dry ingredients, mix them in once more into the dry ingredients.

3. Split the batter amongst the donut tray molds. Bake for 16 to 18 minutes at 335°F in a preheated oven.

4. Once taken off of the trays, let the donuts cool for ten minutes.

5. Fry the donuts on all sides in a skillet with coconut oil that has been heated to a smoking temperature. Using paper towels, drain them.

6. Beat together the heavy cream, butter, cream cheese, vanilla, and powdered erythritol until it gets fluffy. Add in the food coloring, then mix once more and frost the donuts.

Nutritional Information:

Calories: 150

Net Carbs: 2g

Fat: 15g

Protein: 2g

Brownie Muffins For Ketoheads

Serves: 6

Ingredients:

- 1 cup golden flaxseed meal
- ¼ cup cocoa powder
- 1 tbsp. cinnamon
- ½ tsp. salt
- ½ tsp. baking powder 1 egg
- ¼ cup sugar-free caramel syrup
- 2 tbsp. coconut oil
- ½ cup pumpkin purée
- 1 tbsp. apple cider vinegar
- 1 tbsp. vanilla extract
- ¼ cup slivered almonds

Instructions:

1. Turn the oven on to 350°F.

2. In a large mixing bowl, add all the ingredients (except the almonds) and mix thoroughly.

3. Divide the batter into 6 pieces and fill each slot in a prepared muffin tray.

4. Top with a sprinkling of almonds.

5. Bake for approximately fifteen minutes.

Nutritional Information:

Calories: 185

Net Carbs: 3.5g

Fat: 13.5g

Protein: 7.4g

Cheddar Scrambled Eggs With Spinach

Serves: 1.

Ingredients:

- 4 cup fresh spinach
- ½ cup cheddar cheese
- 4 eggs
- tbsp. heavy cream
- tbsp. olive oil
- Salt and pepper

Instructions:

1. Combine the eggs, heavy cream, salt, and pepper in a bowl.

2. Once the olive oil is hot, add the spinach to a big pan.

3. Add the salt and pepper after stirring the spinach.

4. Turn the heat down to medium and stir in the egg mixture once the spinach has wilted somewhat.

5. Add the cheese when the eggs are set, and stir gently until the cheese melts.

Nutritional Information:

Calories: 700

Net Carbs: 5g

Fat: 58g

Protein: 43g

Sausage And Bacon Bite Sized Breakfasts

Serves: 1

Ingredients:

- 6 slices bacon
- 1 tbsp. butter
- 6 oz. breakfast sausage
- ½ tbsp. olive oil

- 6 eggs
- ¾ stalk celery
- ⅕ onion
- 2 stalks leek
- Salt and pepper

Instructions:

1. Combine the sausage and bacon in a food processor. Fill each cup of the mixture to the brim in a cupcake tray, leaving a little indentation on top of each cup. Bake at 375°F for 15 minutes.

2. Finely chop the celery and leeks, then combine them with the greased pan. Add pepper and salt for seasoning. Cook until the leeks and celery are somewhat soft. After removing the mixture from the pan, cook the eggs in the remaining butter.

3. Remove the oven-baked sausage bites. After using a paper towel to remove any extra oil, bake for another ten minutes.

4. After removing the baskets, stuff the onion-leek mixture, place the fried egg on top and serve.

Nutritional Information:

Calories: 239

Net Carbs: 2g

Fat: 20g

Protein: 15g

Versatile Oopsie Rolls

Serves: 6

Ingredients:

- Cooking spray
- 6 eggs
- 6 oz. cream cheese, cold and cubed
- ¼ tsp. salt
- ¼ tsp. cream of tartar

Instructions:

1. Separate the yolks and egg whites. Using an electric hand mixer, whisk the whites until they are foamy.

2. Stir in the cream of tartar and continue to mix until firm peaks begin to form.

3. Gently incorporate the white egg mixture into the smooth combination of egg yolks and cream cheese that has been combined in a separate bowl.

4. Spread the batter onto a parchment---paper-lined cookie sheet.

5. After baking for 30 to 40 minutes, allow it to cool.

Nutritional Information:

Calories: 45

Net Carbs: 0g

Fat: 4g

Protein: 2.5g

Keto Crepes With Blueberries
Serves: 6

Ingredients:

For the Crepe Batter:

- 2 oz. cream cheese
- 10 drops liquid stevia
- 2 eggs
- ¼ tsp. cinnamon

- ⅛ tsp. salt
- ¼ tsp. baking soda

For the Filling:

- 4 oz. cream cheese
- 2 tsp. powdered erythritol
- ½ tsp. vanilla extract
- ½ cup blueberries

Instructions:

1. Using an electric hand mixer, blend the cream cheese and eggs in a bowl until they are smooth.

2. Stir in the salt, baking soda, cinnamon, and stevia.

3. In a nonstick pan, add butter or coconut oil and cook over medium heat. Add enough batter to form a very thin layer, then cook for three minutes. After cooking for an additional minute, flip the crepe and remove it.

4. To prepare the filling, blend cream cheese, vanilla extract, and powdered erythritol together using an electric

mixer until a creamy consistency is achieved.

5. After adding the blueberries, cinnamon, and filling to your crepes, fold or roll them up.

Nutritional Information:

Calories: 400

Net Carbs: 6g

Fat: 35g

Protein: 15g

Italian Sausage And Egg Scramble
Serves: 1.

Ingredients:

- 1 cup red bell pepper, chopped
- 4 eggs
- 1 cup onion, chopped
- 3 spicy Italian chicken sausages
- ¼ cup mozzarella cheese, shredded powder
- Salt

- 1 tsp. cayenne pepper

Instructions:

1. Add the onion and chopped red bell peppers to a pan. Add the chopped chicken sausage and continue to sauté until the onion begins to become translucent.

2. Sauté the sausage for just enough time to warm it up.

3. Using a spatula, combine the eggs and mozzarella cheese.

4. Cook the mixture for a further three to four minutes, or until it is thoroughly cooked.

5. Taste and add the salt and cayenne pepper.

Nutritional Information:

Calories: 750

Net Carbs: 17g

Fat: 40g

Protein: 75g

Keto Cheddar and Sage Waffle

Serves: 12

Ingredients:

- 1 ⅓ cups coconut flour
- 1 tsp. ground sage, dried
- 3 tbsp. baking powder
- ½ tsp. salt
- 2 cups canned coconut milk
- ¼ tsp. garlic powder
- ½ cup water 2 eggs
- 1 cup cheddar cheese, shredded
- 3 tbsp. coconut oil, melted

Instructions:

1. In a bowl, combine the flour, baking powder, and spices.

2. Beat in the coconut oil, water, and coconut milk until a stiff batter forms.

3. Mix in the cheese.

4. Pour ⅓ cup of the batter onto each iron area after preheating and greasing the waffle iron.

5. When the waffles are golden, close the iron.

Nutritional Information:

Calories: 214

Net Carbs: 3.8g

Fat: 17.2g

Protein: 6.5g

Breakfast Burgers

Serves: 2.

Ingredients:

- 4 oz. sausage
- 4 slices bacon
- 2 oz. pepper jack cheese
- 2 eggs
- 1 tbsp. peanut butter powder
- 1 tbsp. butter
- Salt and pepper

Instructions:

1. Place the bacon on a baking sheet and bake for 20 to 25 minutes at 400°F.

2. In a small bowl, mix together the butter and peanut butter powder.

3. Shape the sausage into two patties and cook them thoroughly.

4. To4. To4. To ensure the cheese melts, add it and cover with a lid. Take it out of the pan.

5. Cook the egg and place it on top of the burger with the bacon slices and peanut butter mixture.

Nutritional Information:

Calories: 652

Net Carbs: 3g

Fat: 55g

Protein: 30g

Keto Casserole For Breakfast
Serves: 8

Ingredients:

- ¼ cup flaxseed meal
- 10 eggs
- 1 lb. breakfast sausage
- cup almond flour
- 4 oz. cheese
- ¼ tsp. sage Salt and pepper

- 6 tbsp. light maple syrup
- ½ tsp. onion powder
- 4 tbsp. butter
- ½ tsp. garlic powder

Instructions:

1. Add the morning sausage to a skillet over medium heat and stir often until browned.

2. Combine the sage, onion powder, garlic powder, almond flour, and flaxseed in a bowl.

3. Add in the cheese and eggs into the bowl and stir.

4. Combine this blend with the sausage.

5. Pour the casserole mix into a casserole dish that has been lined with parchment paper. Pour in the two tablespoons. of syrup above.

6. Bake for 45 to 55 minutes at 350°F, then let cool.

Nutritional Information:

Calories: 480

Net Carbs: 3g

Fat: 41.2g

Protein: 22.7g

Peanut Butter Muffins With Chocolate Chips

Serves: 2.

Ingredients:

- ½ cup erythritol
- 1 tbsp. baking powder
- 1 cup almond flour
- ⅓ cup peanut butter 2 eggs
- ⅓ cup almond milk
- ½ cup sugar-free chocolate chips
- Salt

Instructions:

1. In a bowl, whisk together the erythritol, almond flour, and baking powder.

2. Stir in the almond milk and peanut butter.

3. Add in the initial egg and mix thoroughly. Add the second the mix thoroughly.

3. Add the chocolate chips and fold.

4. After putting the muffins in a six-cup muffin tin and baking them for fifteen minutes at 350°F, allow them to cool.

Nutritional Information:

Calories: 527

Net Carbs: 4.3g

Fat: 40g

Protein: 14g

Keto Oatmeal

Serves: 2.

Ingredients:

- ¼ cup shredded coconut, unsweetened
- ¼ cup chia seeds
- ⅓ cup almonds, flaked
- ⅓ cup flaked coconut, unsweetened
- 1 cup hot water

- 1 tsp. unsweetened vanilla extract
- ½ cup coconut milk
- 6-8 drops stevia extract
- 2 tbsp. erythritol

Instructions:

1. Almonds, chia seeds, flakes and shredded coconut should all be combined in a bowl; reserve a little portion of the flaked and almond mixture.

2. Stir in the stevia, vanilla essence, and coconut milk. After adding boiling water, wait ten to fifteen minutes.

3. Top with berries (optional) and scatter almonds and shredded coconut on top.

Nutritional Information:

Calories: 360

Net Carbs: 5 g

Fat: 30 g

Protein: 9.5 g

Keto Green Smoothie

Serves: 1.

Ingredients:

- 1½ cups almond milk
- ⅓ cup cucumber, diced
- 1 oz. spinach
- ⅓ cup celery, diced
- ½ cup avocado, diced
- ¼ cup protein powder
- 1 tbsp. coconut oil
- Liquid stevia

Instructions:

1. In a blender, combine the spinach and almond milk.

2. To create a smooth consistency, add the other ingredients and combine once more.

Nutritional Information:

Calories: 370

Net Carbs: 5g

Fat: 24g

Protein: 27g

Carrot Muffins

Serves: 9.

Ingredients:

For the Cheesetake Layer:

- ¾ cup cream cheese
- 2 tbsp. erythritol
- 1 egg yolk
- 1 tsp. unsweetened vanilla extract

For the rest:

- ½ cup almond flour
- 1 tbsp. ground chia seeds
- 2 tbsp. coconut flour
- ¼ cup Erythritol
- 2 tsp. gluten-free baking powder
- ⅛ tsp. each ground allspice and nutmeg
- 1 tsp. each cinnamon, vanilla powder and ground ginger

- ½ cup chopped pecans 5 egg whites
- ¾ cup carrots, grated 20 drops liquid stevia
- ⅓ cup virgin coconut oil, melted
- Melted coconut oil for greasing
- Salt

Instructions:

1. Combine the cream cheese, egg yolk, erythritol, and vanilla powder to make the cheesecake layer.

2. Mix all of the dry ingredients (except the pecans) thoroughly in another bowl.

3. Put the four egg yolks and the leftover egg white from the cheesecake layer, along with the melted coconut oil and stevia into a large bowl. Stir thoroughly, then gradually add the dry ingredients and stir again.

4. Beat 4 egg whites in a separate bowl until stiff peaks form.

5. Mix the batter gently with ¼ of the egg whites. Using a spatula, carefully fold in the remaining portion. Keeping

the batter as airy as possible, add the pecans and carrot.

6. Spoon the batter into a muffin tray lined with nine muffin paper cups. Give each one a generous tablespoon on top. of the cheesecake batter. Bake at 320°F for 30 to 35 minutes. Take it out and let it cool.

Nutritional Information:

Calories: 270

Net Carbs: 3.7g

Fat: 26g

Protein: 7g

Quick Keto Scramble

Serves: 1.

Ingredients:

- 3 eggs, whisked
- ¼ cup red bell peppers
- 4 baby bella mushrooms
- ½ cup spinach
- 1 tbsp. coconut oil
- 2 slices deli ham

- Salt and pepper

Instructions:

1. Chop the ham and veggies finely.

2. Melted butter in a frying pan helps to brown them.

3. Scramble the eggs until they are fully cooked after adding the seasonings and eggs.

Nutritional Information:

Calories: 350

Net Carbs: 5g

Fat: 30g

Protein: 20g

Savory Delicious Bacon Muffins
Serves: 16

Ingredients:

- 5 eggs
- ½ cups almond flour
- 5 bacon slices

- 2 tbsp. butter
- ¼ cup flaxseed meal
- 2 avocados
- 1½ tbsp. psyllium husk powder
- 4.5 oz. Colby-Jack cheese
- 1 tsp. garlic
- 3bspring onions
- 1 tsp. dried chives
- 1 tsp. cilantro
- 1 ½ cups coconut milk
- ¼ tsp. red chili flakes
- 1 ½ tbsp. lemon juice
- Salt and pepper
- 1 tsp. baking powder

Instructions:

1. Mix the eggs, psyllium, flax, almond flour, lemon juice, spices and coconut milk in a bowl.

2. Melt the butter in a hot skillet and fry the bacon until it's crispy and browned. Take it out, allow it to cool a little, then cut it into little pieces.

3. To the batter, add the avocado, bacon, and remaining ingredients

(including the bacon fat). Mix thoroughly.

3. Pour the batter into 12 well-greased cupcake molds and bake for 20 to 25 minutes at 350°F. Take out and bake the final four muffins.

Nutritional Information:

Calories: 165

Net Carbs: 1.5g

Fat: 14g

Protein: 6g

Keto Banana Pancake

Serves: 4

Ingredients:

- 2 eggs
- 2 tbsp. cashew nuts, ground
- 1 banana
- ¼ tsp. cinnamon
- 1 tbsp. extra virgin coconut oil
- ¼ tsp. ground cloves

For the Topping:

- ¼ tsp. cinnamon
- 3 tbsp. coconut cream

Instructions:

1. In a small bowl, whisk the eggs.

2. Mash the bananas with ground cloves, cashew nuts, and cinnamon in a separate bowl. Completely incorporate the eggs into the mixture.

3. Pour enough batter onto a greased pan, preheat, and cook the pancakes until they are the size of a hand. When the top begins to bubble and the edges start to brown, flip the dish.

4. Once cooked, take it out and sprinkle the cinnamon and coconut cream on top.

Nutritional Information:

Calories: 585

Net Carbs: 27g

Fat: 45g

Protein: 20g

Little Red Chocolate Cakes

Serves: 1.

Ingredients:

- 1 tbsp. coconut flour
- 3 tbsp. erythritol
- ⅓ cup almond flour
- 1 tbsp. unsweetened cocoa powder
- ¼ tsp. baking soda
- 2 eggs
- ¼ tsp. vanilla powder
- ¼ cup sour cream
- 1 tbsp. beetroot powder
- 2 tbsp. extra virgin coconut oil

For the Frosting:

- 2 tbsp. butter, room temperature
- 1 tbsp. powdered erythritol
- ¼ cup cream cheese
- ¼ tsp. vanilla powder

Instructions:

1. Almond flour, coconut flour, baking soda, erythritol, cacao powder, and beetroot powder should all be combined in a bowl.

2. Mix thoroughly after adding the sour cream, eggs, and melted coconut oil.

3. Transfer the blend into a pair of cups. For 70–90 seconds, microwave each of them on high.

4. In the meantime, beat together the butter, cream cheese, vanilla, and erythritol to make the frosting.

5. Enjoy your final mug cakes with frosting.

Nutritional Information:

Calories: 560

Net Carbs: 8g

Fat: 55g

Protein: 15g

Keto French Toast

Serves: 2 loaves

Ingredients:

- 14 eggs, separated

- 4 oz. cream cheese, softened
- 1 cup whey protein
- 1 cup unsweetened almond milk
- 1 tsp. cinnamon
- 1 tsp. vanilla
- ½ cup butter
- ½ cup Granulated sweetener of your choice

Instructions:

1. To make the bread, beat 12 egg whites until firm peaks form, about 10 minutes. Gently whisk in the whey protein before folding in the cream cheese.

2. Pour the batter into two bread pans that have been greased. Bake at 325°F for approximately 40–45 minutes. Take them out and let them cool. After they cool fully, slice them to the desired thickness.

3. In a bowl, whisk together 2 eggs, ½ cup unsweetened almond milk, cinnamon, and vanilla. Slices of bread are dipped in the mixture.

4. After placing the bread on a skillet, grill it until it gets a light brown color on both sides. Continue with the remaining ones.

5. To make the sauce, put a skillet over high heat with the butter. Once it starts to boil and become brown, mix in the sweetener and the remaining ½ cup of almond milk into the skillet. Mix well and rapidly pour into a recipient. Let it cool in the pan for a few minutes. Place it on top of the toast.

Nutritional Information:

Calories: 125

Net Carbs: 0.7g

Fat: 15g

Protein: 6.5g

Lunch Recipes
Keto Chicken Salad

Time: 5 minutes

Serving Size: Serves 2

Ingredients:

- ¼ tsp salt
- ⅓ cup mayo
- tbsp fresh chives
- tbsp fresh dill
- 1 tbsp Dijon mustard
- tbsp red onion (finely chopped)
- ¼ cup bacon (crumbled)
- ¼ tsp fresh ground black pepper
- 2 cups cooked chicken breast (shredded)
- ½ cup celery (finely chopped)

Instructions:

1. Before you start, properly cook and shred the chicken breast.

2. Once you have mixed the salt, mayo, pepper, mustard, dill, and chives, create your dressing in a bowl.

3. Add the chicken, red onion, bacon, and celery the minute you start your dressing.

4. Mix thoroughly.

5. To give it a taste, sprinkle some salt and pepper.

Nutritional Information:

Kcal - 366

Protein - 18 g

Fat - 30 g

Net Carbs - 2 g

Keto Tacos

Time: 20 minutes

Serving Size: Serves 4

Ingredients:

- 1.1lb. ground beef

- tbsp tomato puree (unsweetened)
- 4 low-carb taco shells
- ½ tsp ground cumin
- Cloves of garlic
- medium avocado
- Freshly ground cayenne pepper or ground black pepper
- 1 tsp chili powder
- 1 cup cherry tomatoes
- 1 white onion (finely chopped)

- 1 tbsp extra virgin coconut oil
- 1 cup water
- 1 small lettuce
- ½ tsp salt

Instructions:

1. Prepare the taco shells on a plate.

2. Remove the outer layer of the onions and cut them alongside the garlic.

3. Put the onion and garlic in a pan set over coconut oil.

4. Cook the onion and garlic on an ordinary (middle to high) heat, stirring now and again until brown.

5. Add the ground meat and heat until all sides are brown.

6. Add the chili powder and cumin; properly combine.

7. Add the unsweetened tomato puree, and then pour the water into it.

8. Taste the mixture with salt and pepper and well stir it.

9. Cook until the meat is cooked and the sauce lowers, some more minutes.

10. Place the meat and sauce aside.

11. With a paper towel, wash and dry the vegetables.

12. Chop the lettuce, avocado, and tomatoes in tiny bits.

13. Load the shells with the mixture.

14. Make use of Avocado, lettuce, and tomato as toppings or use any other alternative keto diet topping on the keto meal list.

Nutritional Information:

Net carbs - 6.6 g

Fiber - 10.6 g

Fat - 54.3 g

Protein - 28.6 g

Kcal - 658

Spicy Cauliflower Soup

Time: 20 minutes

Serving Size: Serves 6

Ingredients:

- 3 tbsp butter
- medium Spanish chorizo sausage
- white onion (finely chopped)
- 1 large cauliflower
- 1 medium spring onion
- ½ tsp salt
- cups vegetable stock, chicken stock, or bone broth
- 1 medium turnip

Instructions:

1. Rinse and clean the cauliflower in a properly.

2. On a chopping board, place the cauliflower and cut it into little pieces.

3. Get a Dutch oven, then oil with two tablespoons of butter, then add the onion. Cook it over medium-high heat until it turns brown.

4. Add the chopped cauliflower from step two above.

5. Leave it to cook for roughly five minutes, stirring often.

6. Add the stock, then cover the pot to seal it.

7. Set it to cook for ten minutes.

8. Chop up the sausage.

9. Peel off the sides of the turnip and chop it finely.

10. Arrange the pre-cut and peeled items on an oiled skillet with the remaining butter.

11. Average (medium to high) heat should be used to cook the sausage and

chorizo for 8 to 10 minutes until the sausage gets crispy and the chorizo becomes soft.

12. Put half of the chorizo and turnip mixture, in the pot holding the soup.

13. Use a blender to correctly combine until it becomes creamy and smooth.

14. Spoon the soup into a bow.

15. Drizzle with the remaining turnip and chorizo combination, and add a tiny bit of hot oil to give it a fiery taste.

16. Top with the chopped spring onion.

Nutritional Information:

Protein - 10.7 g

Net Carbs - 7 g

Fiber - 3.6 g

Kcal - 251

Fat - 19.1 g

Keto Mexican Rice w/ Chorizo

Time: 20 minutes

Serving Size: Serves 4

Ingredients:

- 5 cups cauliflower rice (made from 1 cauliflower head)
- pinch of sea salt
- 6 to 8 jalapeno peppers
- 4 tbsp parsley (chopped)
- chorizo sausages
- tbsp butter

Instructions:

1. Give the cauliflower a good wash.

2. Remove its leaves and strong core, then cut it.

3. Using a food processor, pulse the florets until they resemble rice. You might grate it with the manual hand grater as another option.

4. Keep the cauliflower rice you will later use in a sealed jar for four days.

5. Take some of your cauliflower rice.

6. Chop the chorizo finely and cut off the seed from the jalapeño peppers.

7. Oil a skillet; then, add peppers and chorizo.

8. Cook until both are brown. Try to whisk the mixture at least two times.

9. Add the cauliflower rice and cook for five to ten minutes to reach your desired softness.

10. Add parsley first, then seasonings (salt) to taste.

Nutritional Information:

Fiber - 3.7 g

Kcal - 386

Net Carbs - 6.4 g

Fat - 31 g

Protein - 17.6 g

Zucchini Noodles w/ Pesto
Time: 20 minutes

Serving Size: Serves 4

Ingredients:

- ¼ tsp salt
- ½ cup pesto
- 4 zucchini
- ½ tbsp olive oil
- cup cherry tomatoes (quartered)

Instructions:

1. Wash the zucchini properly.

2. Cut out the latter portion of the zucchini and gently separate it into strands like spaghetti using a spiralizer (tabletop).

3. After sprinkling olive oil, add the noodles to a large pot or skillet.

4. Heat the noodles, it should start to turn tender after three to four minutes on an average (medium) heat.

5. Add the pesto and tomatoes.

6. Cook for a minimum of 2 minutes.

7. Take it off the stove and serve it.

Nutritional Information:

kcal - 246

Net Carbs - 10 g

Fiber - 3 g

Fat - 22 g

Protein - 3 g

Keto Deviled Eggs

Time: 15 minutes

Serving Size: Serves 4

Ingredients:

- pinch herbal salt
- dill (fresh)
- ¼ cup mayo
- 8 peeled shrimps (cooked)
- 4 medium eggs
- tsp Tabasco

Instructions:

1. Place the eggs in a pot and filling it with water, cover it.

2. On medium heat, allow the water to boil.

3. Boil for about eight to ten minutes.

4. Take out the eggs from the pot and spend several minutes in the water-filled basin.

5. Peel the eggs, then divide them in two.

6. Remove the yolks, then arrange the egg whites on a plate.

7. Stuck the yolk with a fork.

8. Add Tabasco, mayo, and herbal salt to the mixture.

9. Using two spoons, scoop a portion of the mixture; then, arrange on the egg whites.

10. Top the egg whites with grilled prawns.

11. Add dill to garnish the meal.

Nutritional Information:

Fiber - 0 g

Fat - 15 g

Net Carbs - 0.5 g

Protein - 7 g

Kcal - 163

Keto Cashew Chicken

Time: 20 to 25 minutes

Serving Size: Serves 3

Ingredients:

- 3 chicken thighs
- tbsp minced garlic
- ½ tbsp chili garlic sauce

- ½ medium green bell pepper
- ½ tbsp rice wine vinegar
- ½ tsp ground ginger
- ½ tsp liquid aminos
- ¼ cup raw cashews
- 1 tbsp sesame oil
- Salt & pepper
- 1 tbsp green onions
- ¼ white onion
- tbsp coconut oil

Instructions:

1. On a stove, place and heat a pan over low heat.

2. Arrange the cashews in the pan and roast them till just brown—about 8 minutes.

3. Take off toasted cashews then put aside.

4. Cut the chicken thighs one inch apart.

5. Chop the onion and pepper somewhat large.

6. Turn on the heat and pour coconut oil into the pan.

7. Once the oil is at a moderate temperature, put in the chicken thighs and cook for around five minutes.

8. Add the onions, pepper, chili garlic sauce, garlic, and other seasonings once the chicken thighs have been properly cooked.

9. Mix properly and let it cook on high heat for two to three minutes.

10. Combine the liquid aminos, rice wine vinegar, and cashews while you cook on high heat.

11. Cook the liquid till it begins to become sticky.

12. Remove from the heat and set in a bowl.

13. Add the sesame seeds and oil to enhance the flavor.

Nutritional Information:

kcal - 333.3

Net Carbs - 6.7 g

Fat - 24 g

Protein - 22.6 g

Fiber - 1.3g

Shrimp Tacos w/ Mango Avocado Salsa

Time: 20 minutes

Serving Size: Serves 12

Ingredients:

SHRIMP

- lb large shrimp (peeled and stripped)

- ½ tsp cumin
- ¼ tsp ancho chilli powder
- ½ tsp smoked paprika
- ⅛ tsp sea salt
- ¼ tsp garlic powder

TACTOS

- 10 to 12 butter lettuce leaves
- yellow pepper (julienned)
- red pepper (julienned)
- 1 tbsp olive oil
- Salt
- ¼ cup chopped cilantro; lime juice

MANGO AVOCADO SALSA MIX

- 3 avocados (diced)
- salt (for taste)
- ¾ cup mango (diced)
- ¼ cup red onion (diced)
- tbsp red wine vinegar
- ½ tbsp diced jalapeno
- lime juice
- ¼ cup cilantro (chopped)

Instructions:

1. Preheat the grill and ensure its moderate hot at about 400°F or 200°C.

2. In a bowl, properly mix the lime juice, avocado, chopped mango, red onion, jalapeno, cilantro, salt, and red wine vinegar.

3. In another small bowl, whisk together the cumin, garlic powder, smoked paprika, ancho chili powder, and ½ teaspoon salt.

4. Marinate the peppers with olive oil and salt.

5. Add the spice bled to the shrimp's seasonings.

6. Apply cooking spray to the pan.

7. Spoon the pepper from step 4 above straight onto the pan.

8. Cook them for about four to five minutes, until the peppers start to turn slightly browned.

9. Remove the scorched peppers from the grill and arrange them in a in a large bowl.

10. Sear the seasoned prawns on the grill pan for two to three minutes on each side.

11. Remove the prawns from the grill pan as they turn pink, and place them in the large bowl with the peppers.

12. Toss and mix everything in the large bowl.

13. Place the peppers and prawns in lettuce cups, then sprinkle your salsa mix to taste.

Nutritional Information:

Fat - 13 g

kcal - 222

Net Carbs - 15 g

Fiber - 7 g

Protein - 21 g

Paleo Sushi Rolls

Time: 15 minutes

Serving Size: Serves 1

Ingredients:

- 1 tablespoon mayo

- 5 ounces salmon (cooked)
- 3 square nori sheets or seaweed wrappers
- ⅓ red pepper (sliced)
- 1 tablespoon spicy sauce.
- 1 spring onion (chopped into two to three-inch pieces)
- 1 teaspoon of white or black sesame seeds
- ½ a cucumber (sliced)
- ½ avocado (sliced)

Instructions:

1. Place the nori sheet on a level surface, with the bright side down.

2. One-third of the nori sheet should have one-third of the fish placed on either the left or right sides.

3. Top it with two slices of cucumbers, avocado and pepper.

4. Add some hot sauce and some green onions to the mayo.

5. From the side you are rolling; moisten the most of the nori sheet at roughly one to two cm.

6. Holding the opposite covering edge of the roll, begin to roll it over the ingredients.

7. Continue to roll the wrapper until the high edge tightly crushes its overlap.

8. Place the roll on a board with the seam facing downward.

9. Cut it into comfortably biteable portions.

10. Keep it in a sealed container, until you are ready to consume it. Before you serve, you could also add more mayo as a seasoning.

Nutritional Information:

Fiber - 8 g

kcal - 556

Net Carbs - 21.5 g

Fat - 36.2 g

Protein - 38.4 g

Keto Bread

Time: 17 minutes

Serving Size: Serves 1

Ingredients:

- ⅛ tsp salt
- tbsp. almond flour
- 1 tablespoon coconut flour
- Butter
- 1 egg
- 1 tbsp. almond milk
- ¼ baking powder

Instructions:

1. Preheat the oven to 400°F (approximately 200°C).

2. Oil a ramekin with butter or cooking spray.

3. Crack the egg and place it in a basin.

4. Beat in salt, almond flour, milk, coconut flour, and butter, stir them thoroughly to ensure they combine smoothly. To enhance the flavor of your bread, add a little cheese and spinach.

5. Return a full spoonful of the mixture prepared a few minutes ago to the ramekin.

6. Bake for approximately 10–15 minutes. Microwave the mixture on high for 1.5 minutes.

7. Remove the ramekin and let it cool for 5 minutes.

8. Turn the ramekins and remove the cooked bread.

Nutritional Information:

Fat, 20 g

kcal - 237

Fiber: 3 g

Net Carbs: 3 g

Protein: 8 g

Keto Meatballs

Time: 20 minutes.

Ingredients: Serves 4 people.

Ingredients:

- ¾ tsp sea salt
- ½ tsp. black pepper
- ¾ oz. parsley
- ¾ tsp. onion powder
- 16 oz. lean ground beef
- ¾ tsp garlic powder

Instructions:

1. Preheat the oven to 400° Fahrenheit, which is approximately 200° Celsius.

2. Arrange parchment paper on a baking pan.

3. Mix the beef, garlic powder, black pepper, sea salt, onion powder, and parsley in a bowl.

4. Spin the meatballs, which should yield around 8, including your mixture, and place them on a baking sheet.

5. Bake the meatballs for 15 to 18 minutes, or until thoroughly cooked.

6. Sprinkle some cheese to add flavor.

Nutritional Information:

Protein: 3.1 g

Fat, 8 g

Net Carbs: -0.7 g

Fibre, 2 g

kcal - 380

"No Chop" Keto Chili

Time: 15 minutes.

Serving Size: Serves 6

Ingredients:

- salt and pepper
- tsp. ground cumin
- ½ cup of salsa
- ½ tsp. garlic powder
- ½ tsp ground cayenne
- tsp. ground coriander
- 1 lb. lean ground beef or turkey

Instructions:

1. Mix the ground beef and spices in a saucepan of medium size.

2. Simmer for a duration of 5 minutes on a medium heat setting, simmer for five minutes.

3. Once the beef mixture is thoroughly cooked, include the salsa.

4. Continue to heat the contents in the saucepan at a low temperature for a further five minutes.

Nutritional Information:

kcal - 229

Fat, 9 g

Fiber - 0 g

Protein (33 g)

Net carbs: 2 g

Easy chopped salad

Serves 1

Prep time: 10 minutes.

Cook Time:--

Ingredients:

- A small head of chopped romaine lettuce
- tablespoons diced red onions
- tablespoons of chopped fresh mint
- ¼ cup (60 ml) vinaigrette of choice
- 8 cherry or grape tomatoes, halved
- ½ cucumber, seeded and chopped
- celery stick, chopped
- ¼ cup (45 g) pitted black olives, chopped

Instructions:

Place the lettuce in a large serving basin. Use the remaining salad ingredients to top, then drizzle with the vinaigrette and enjoy.

Nutritional Information:

Calories: 476

Fat:79%

Protein:5%

Carbs:15%

Chili-lime chicken bowls

Serves 4

Prep time: 15 minutes.

Cook time: 30 minutes.

Ingredients:

CILANTRO CAULIFLOWER RICE SALAD

- 2 tablespoons of lime juice
- 2 Chopped green onions
- ½ teaspoon finely powdered sea salt
- ¼ teaspoon ground black pepper
- ¼ cup (60 ml) avocado oil
- medium-head cauliflower (approximately 1½ lbs/680 g) or 3 cups (375 g). Pre-riced cauliflower
- ⅓ packed cup (27 g) of chopped fresh cilantro leaves and stems

CHILI LIME CHICKEN:

Ingredients:

- 2 tablespoons of avocado oil
- ½ teaspoon paprika
- ¾ teaspoon ground cumin
- teaspoons erythritol
- tablespoon of lime juice
- 1½ teaspoons chili powder
- teaspoon garlic powder

- teaspoons of hot sauce
- ¼ teaspoon ground black pepper
- 1 pound (455 g) of boneless, skinless chicken thighs
- ¾ teaspoon finely ground sea salt

Instructions:

1. If you want to use pre-riced cauliflower, go to Step 2.

2. If not, slice off the base of the cauliflower head and remove the florets. Transfer the florets to a blender and pulse 3 to 4 times to break them into small bits.

3. Put the riced cauliflower in a large pot and fill it with water. Seal the lid and bring to a boil over high heat, then reduce to a simmer and cook for 5 minutes, or until soft but not mushy. After that, drain the cauliflower by squeezing it with the back of a spoon to remove as much water as you can. Transfer the drained cauliflower to a large mixing bowl and place it in the refrigerator to cool.

4. Prepare the chili lime chicken, then combine all of the ingredients, except the chicken thighs, in a large frying pan. Whisk until properly combined, then add the chicken and toss to coat. Close the lid or cover and cook at low heat for 25 minutes, or until the chicken reaches an internal temperature of 165°F.

5. After about 20 minutes, bring out the cooked cauliflower from the refrigerator, then mix in the remaining ingredients for the cauliflower rice salad. Toss to coat, then divide evenly among 4 bowls. Top each bowl with ¼ of the chili lime chicken and a small quantity of the pan sauce. Serve!

Nutritional Information:

Calories: 268

Protein: 38%

Carbs: 16%

Fat: 46%

Salmon salad cups

Serves: 4

Prep time: 10 minutes.

Cook Time:

Ingredients:

- 12 ounces (340 g) of canned salmon (no salt added)
- 1/2 cup (105 g) mayonnaise
- 3 tablespoons of prepared horseradish
- Twelve butter lettuce leaves (from one head)
- Three tablespoons of minced fresh dill
- 1/2 teaspoon finely ground sea salt
- a teaspoon of lemon juice.
- 1/2 teaspoon ground black pepper

Instructions:

1. Place the salmon, horseradish, pepper, salt, dill, and lemon juice in a medium-sized bowl. Stir until the ingredients are completely blended.

2. Place the lettuce leaves on a plate. Fill each leaf with two tablespoons of the

salmon salad solution, then add two teaspoons of mayonnaise for topping.

Nutritional Information:

Calories: 314

Fat:76%

Carbs:6%

Protein:19%

Steak-fried cups

Serves: 6

Prep time: 10 minutes, plus 2 hours for marinating.

Cooking time: 8 minutes

Ingredients:

- ¼ cup plus 2 tablespoons (90 ml) of avocado oil
- ½ teaspoon ground black pepper
- 1 Diced red onion
- ¼ cup (60 ml) coconut aminos
- 6 cloves garlic, minced
- 2 tablespoons of hot sauce
- yellow bell pepper, sliced

- 2 tablespoons of lime juice
- ¼ cup (17 g) of chopped fresh parsley leaves
- 1 pound (455 g) top sirloin steak, cubed
- 36 endive leaves (from about 6 heads of endive)

Instructions:

1. Combine the black pepper, lime juice, oil, coconut aminos, spicy sauce, and garlic in a medium-sized bowl. Whisk together, then add the bell pepper, onion, and steak, tossing to combine. Seal the bowl and chill for at least 120 minutes to marinate.

2. When ready to cook the steak, transfer the entire contents of the bowl to a large frying pan. Cook over medium heat for about 8 minutes, stirring frequently, until the steak is thoroughly cooked.

3. Meanwhile, distribute evenly. Divide the endive leaves among six plates. When serving, fill each leaf with two

tablespoons of steak solution. Drizzle with parsley and enjoy.

Nutritional Information:

Calories: 325

Fat: 53%

Protein: 32%

Carbs: 15%

Antipasto Salad

Serves 4

Prep time: 10 minutes.

Cook Time:

Ingredients:

- (12-oz/340-g) jar roasted red peppers, drained and roughly chopped
- ¾ cup (210 ml) vinaigrette of choice
- 3 tablespoons capers, drained
- 1 (6½-oz/185-g) jar marinated artichoke quarters, drained and roughly chopped

- 1 (4-oz/113-g) can sliced cremini mushrooms, drained
- 4 Ounces (115 g) salami, sliced

Instructions:

Place all of the ingredients in a large mixing basin. Toss to coat and serve.

Nutritional Information:

Calories: 433.

Carbs: 12%

Fat: 81%

Protein: 7%

German no-tato salad

Serves: 5.

Prep time: 10 minutes.

Cook time: 10 minutes.

Ingredients:

- 1 teaspoon finely ground sea salt
- 2 medium peeled rutabaga (2 lbs/910 g)

- 4 sliced green onions
- ¼ cup (60 ml) avocado oil or olive oil
- 1 finely diced red onion
- ¼ cup (60 ml) apple cider vinegar
- ¾ teaspoon ground black pepper
- 1 tablespoon Dijon mustard
- 1 teaspoon erythritol

FOR SERVING:

- 1 tablespoon plus 2 teaspoons mayonnaise
- 10 ounces (285 g) thinly sliced deli ham or other meat of choice
- 1 tablespoon plus 2 teaspoons Dijon mustard

Instructions:

1. Cut the rutabaga into ½-inch cubes, set in a large saucepan, cover with water, and add salt. Seal with a lid, bring to a boil over high heat, then reduce to a simmer and cook for 10 minutes until soft.

2. Meanwhile, mix all of the remaining ingredients in a large salad bowl. Once the rutabaga is cooked, drain it fully and

transfer it to a salad bowl. Toss it to combine, then divide among 5 plates.

3. Combine the mayonnaise and mustard in a small bowl.

4. Serve the ham slices with the salad and two teaspoons of mustard sauce.

Nutritional Information:

Calories: 296

Fat:57%

Carbs:25%

Protein:19%

Broccoli Ginger Soup

Serves: 4

Prep time: 5 minutes.

Cooking time: 25 minutes

Ingredients:

- 2 cloves garlic, minced
- 3 tablespoons coconut oil or avocado oil

- 1 small white onion, sliced
- 1½ teaspoons turmeric powder
- 1½ cups (355 ml) chicken bone broth
- ¾ teaspoon finely ground sea salt
- ¼ cup (40 g) sesame seeds
- 5 cups (420 g) broccoli florets
- ⅓ cup (55 g) collagen peptides (optional)
- 1 (2-in/5-cm) piece fresh ginger root, peeled and minced
- 1 (13½-oz/400-ml) can full-fat coconut milk

Instructions:

1. Heat the oil in a large frying pan over medium heat. Cook the garlic and onion for 10 minutes, or until they are transparent.

2. Combine turmeric, broccoli, broth, coconut milk, ginger, and salt. Close the lid and heat for 15 minutes, or until the broccoli is cooked.

3. Transfer the broccoli mixture into a blender. Add the collagen if desired, and blend until fully smooth.

4. Divide among four bowls and top with a tablespoon of sesame seeds. Serve and enjoy!

Nutritional information:

Calories: 344

Fat: 70%

Carbs: 14%

Protein: 15%

Sauerkraut Soup

Serves: 4

Prep time: 2 minutes.

Cooking time: 25 minutes

Ingredients:

- 1 pound (455 g) ground beef
- 1 small white onion, thinly sliced
- ½ teaspoon finely ground sea salt
- 1 cup (235 g) sauerkraut
- 3 cups (710 ml) beef bone broth
- 1 clove garlic, minced
- 1¼ teaspoons ground cumin

Instructions:

1. Combine cumin, ground meat, garlic, and onion in a saucepan. Place over moderate (middle) heat for approximately 10 minutes, or until the onion is transparent.

2. Combine the broth, salt, and sauerkraut. Seal and cook over medium heat for about 15 minutes, or until the onion is tender and the soup is fragrant.

3. Evenly split the soup into four dishes and serve.

Nutrition Information:

Calories: 469

CARBS: 7%

Fat: 52%

PROTEIN: 42%

Zucchini Boats

Serves: 1

Ingredients:

- 2 tbsp. butter
- 2 large zucchini

- 3 oz. shredded cheddar cheese
- 2 tbsp. sour cream
- 1 cup broccoli
- 6 oz. shredded rotisserie chicken
- 1 stalk green onion
- Salt and pepper

Instructions:

1. Slice the zucchini lengthwise in half, then remove the center so that the vegetable is shaped like a boat.

2. Drizzle a little melted butter into each zucchini, season, and bake at 400°F for about 18 minutes.

3. Put the chicken, broccoli, and sour cream in a bowl.

4. Stuff the chicken mixture into the zucchini hollows.

5. Add some cheddar cheese on top, then bake for a further ten to fifteen minutes.

Nutritional Information:

Calories: 480

Net Carbs: 5g

Fat: 35g

Protein: 28g

Keto Flat Bread

Serves: 8

Ingredients:

For the crust:

- 2 tbsp. cream cheese
- 2 cups half-and-half grated mozzarella cheese
- ¾ cup almond flour
- ⅛ tsp. dried thyme
- ½ tsp. sea salt

For the topping:

- ½ red onion, small and sliced
- 1 cup grated Mexican cheese
- 4 oz. low carbohydrate sliced ham, cut
- ⅛ tsp. thyme, dried
- Salt and pepper
- ¼ medium apple, unpeeled and sliced

Instructions:

1. After adding a small amount of water to a saucepan, bring it to a boil and reduce the heat. To create a double boiler, place the pot inside a metal mixing bowl. Then, add the salt, thyme, almond flour, cream cheese, mozzarella, and cream cheese. Using a spatula, stir.

2. After the cheese has melted, combine the ingredients to form a dough. Transfer a portion onto a 12-inch parchment paper-covered pizza tray. Turn then Place the dough ball in the middle of the parchment paper. To coat the pan, press it into a round shape.

3. Using a fork to make holes in the dough, place the dough and the parchment paper on the pizza pan. Bake at 425°F for 6 to 8 minutes. Take out.

4. Arrange the cheese, ham, apple, and onion among the toppings on the flatbread. Add extra cheese on top. Add thyme, salt, and pepper for seasoning.

5. Bake at 350°F for another 5 to 7 minutes. When the cheese starts to

brown, remove it. Before slicing leave to cool.

Nutritional Information:

Calories: 257

Net Carbs: 5g

Fat: 22g

Protein: 18g

Keto Stromboli

Serves: 4

Ingredients:

- 1¼ cup shredded mozzarella cheese
- 3 tbsp. coconut flour
- 4 tbsp. almond flour
- 1 egg
- 4 oz. ham
- 1 tsp. Italian seasoning
- 4 oz. cheddar cheese Salt and pepper

Instructions:

1. In order to prevent burning, microwave the mozzarella cheese for about a minute, stirring occasionally.

2. Melt the mozzarella cheese and stir in the almond flour, coconut flour, salt, and pepper in a different bowl. Blend thoroughly. Once it has cooled down a little, add the eggs and stir once more.

3. Spoon the mixture onto parchment paper; cover with a second layer. Using your hands or a rolling pin, press it into a rectangular shape.

4. After removing the top layer of paper, cut diagonal lines toward the center of the dough with a knife. On one side, they need to be chopped ⅓ of the way in. Next, make diagonal cuts on the opposite side, too.

5. Place slices of cheese and ham alternately on top of the dough. Next, cover the filling by folding over one edge, then the other.

6. Transfer to a baking sheet and bake for 15 to 20 minutes at 400°F.

Nutritional Information:

Calories: 305

Net Carbs: 5g

Fat: 22g

Protein: 25g

Tuna Bites With Avocado

Serves: 8

Ingredients:

- 10 oz. drained canned tuna
- ¼ cup parmesan cheese
- ¼ cup mayo 1 avocado
- ½ tsp. garlic powder
- ⅓ cup almond flour
- ¼ tsp. onion powder
- Salt and pepper
- ½ cup coconut oil

Instructions:

1. Combine all the ingredients (except for the coconut oil) in a bowl. Roll into little balls and coat in almond flour.

2. In a pan over medium heat, melt the coconut oil and fry the coconuts until they appear golden all over.

Nutritional Information:

Calories: 137

Net Carbs: 10g

Fat: 12g

Protein: 6g

Keto Chicken Sandwich

Serves: 2

Ingredients:

For the bread:

- 3 eggs
- Salt
- 3 oz. cream cheese
- Garlic powder
- ⅛ tsp. cream of tartar

For the filling:

- 1 tbsp. mayonnaise
- 2 slices bacon
- 1 tsp. sriracha

- 3 oz. chicken
- 2 slices pepper jack cheese
- ¼ avocado
- 2 grape tomatoes

Instructions:

1. Place the eggs in separate bowls. Add cream tartar and salt to the egg whites and whisk until firm peaks form.

2. Beat the egg yolks and cream cheese in a separate bowl. Carefully combine the mixture with the egg white mixture.

3. Transfer the batter onto a sheet of parchment paper and use it to shape little squares that resemble slices of bread. Add a dusting of garlic powder and bake at 300°F for twenty-five minutes.

4. While the bread bakes, cook the bacon and chicken in a frying pan, seasoning to taste.

5. Take the bread out of the oven and allow it to cool for ten to fifteen minutes. After that, assemble the sandwich by layering the cooked chicken

and bacon with mashed avocado, tomatoes, cheese, mayo, and Sriracha to taste.

Nutritional Information:

Calories: 360

Net Carbs: 3g

Fat: 28g

Protein: 22g

Keto Green Salad

Serves: 1

Ingredients:

- 3 tbsp. roasted pine nuts
- 2 oz. mixed greens
- 2 tbsp. raspberry vinaigrette
- 2 slices bacon
- 2 tbsp. parmesan, shaved
- Salt and pepper

Instructions:

1. Cook in a pan until the bacon is nicely browned and crunchy. Cut into pieces

and combine with the remaining ingredients in a bowl.

2. Pour the raspberry vinaigrette over the salad.

Nutritional Information:

Calories: 480

Net Carbs: 4g

Fat: 37g

Protein: 17g

Easy Egg Soup

Serves: 1

Ingredients:

- 1½ cups chicken broth
- 1 tbsp. bacon fat
- 1 tsp. chili garlic paste
- ½ cube of chicken bouillon
- 2 eggs

Instructions:

1. Place the bacon fat, bouillon cube, and chicken stock in a skillet over medium-high heat on the stove. Bring

to a boil, then stir in the garlic and chili paste.

2. Whisk the eggs into the chicken while stirring them in, then allow it to settle for a few minutes.

Nutritional Information:

Calories: 280

Net Carbs: 2.7g

Fat: 25g

Protein: 13g

Original Keto Stuffed Hot Dogs

Serves: 6

Ingredients:

- 12 slices bacon
- ½ tsp. cheese garlic powder
- 6 hot dogs
- 2 oz. cheddar
- Salt and pepper
- ½ tsp. onion powder

Instructions:

1. Cut a small opening in each hot dog and insert cheese slices inside. Place two bacon slices over one another on each hot dog and fasten with toothpicks.

2. Place the hotdogs on top of a wire rack with a cookie sheet underneath. After seasoning, bake for 20 to 25 minutes at 400°F.

Nutritional Information:

Calories: 385

Net Carbs: 0.5g

Fat: 34g

Protein: 17g

Original Nasi Lemak

Serves: 2

Ingredients:

For the Chitken and Egg:

- 2 chicken thighs, boneless
- 1 egg
- ½ tsp. curry powder

- ½ tsp. lime juice
- ¼ tsp. turmeric powder
- A pinch of salt
- ½ tbsp. coconut oil

For the Nasi Lemak:

- 3 tbsp. coconut milk
- 4 slices cucumber
- 3 slices ginger
- 1 cup riced cauliflower
- Salt
- ½ small shallot

Instructions:

1. After rinsing the cauliflower, drain the liquid.

2. Mix the curry powder, turmeric powder, lemon juice, and salt together, then let the chicken thighs marinade in the refrigerator for one or two hours. Take it out and cook.

3. In a saucepan, bring the coconut milk, shallots, and ginger to a boil. Once it begins to bubble, add the cauliflower rice and stir.

4. Serve alongside the fried egg and marinated fried chicken.

Nutritional Information:

Calories: 502

Net Carbs: 7g

Fat: 40g

Protein: 28g

Mug Cake With Jalapeño

Serves: 1

Ingredients:

- 2 tbsp. almond flour
- 1 tbsp. butter
- 1 tbsp. flaxseed meal
- ½ tsp. baking powder
- 1 tbsp. cream cheese
- 1 bacon slice, cooked
- 1 egg
- ½ jalapeño pepper, sliced
- ¼ tsp. salt

Instructions:

1. In a frying pan over medium heat, cook the bacon until crispy.

2. Combine all the ingredients in a bowl and transfer a portion into a mug. Microwave on high for 75 seconds.

3. Before consuming, carefully remove the mug cake and allow it to cool.

Nutritional Information:

Calories: 430

Net Carbs: 4g

Fat: 40g

Protein: 17g

Keto Sausage And Pepper Soup
Serves: 6

Ingredients:

- 30 oz. pork sausage
- 10 oz. raw spinach
- tbsp. olive oil
- 1 medium green bell pepper
- 4 cups beef stock
- 1 can tomatoes with jalapeños

- 1 tbsp. chili powder
- 1 tbsp. onion powder
- 1 tsp. cumin garlic powder
- Salt
- 1 tsp. Italian seasoning

Instructions:

1. Sausage should be cooked in a big saucepan with hot, medium-high olive oil. Stir.

2. Add the chopped green pepper to the saucepan. Mix thoroughly. Add pepper and salt for seasoning. Include the jalapeños and tomatoes. Stir.

3. Cover the pot and place the spinach on top. Add the spices and broth once they have wilted, and stir.

4. Cover the pot and cook over medium-low heat for approximately half an hour. After it's finished, take off the top and simmer the soup for around ten minutes.

Nutritional Information:

Calories: 525

Net Carbs: 4g

Fat: 45g

Protein: 28g

Original Squash Lasagna

Serves: 12

Ingredients:

- 1 lb. spaghetti squash
- 30 slices mozzarella cheese
- 3 lb. ground beef
- 32 oz. whole milk ricotta cheese
- 1 large jar marinara sauce

Instructions:

1. Split the spaghetti squash in half and put each half, cut-side down, on a baking tray. Pour in about half an inch of water. Bake for forty-five minutes. When you're done, carefully remove the squash's meat.

2. In a frying pan, cook the ground beef with the marinara sauce.

3. Lay the spaghetti squash in a baking pan that has been oiled, then top with

the meat sauce, mozzarella, and ricotta. Continue until the pan is filled.

4. Bake at 375°F for 35 minutes.

Nutritional Information:

Calories: 710

Net Carbs: 17g

Fat: 60g

Protein: 45g

Fresh Keto Sandwich

Serves: 1

Ingredients:

- 1 cucumber
- Meat of your choice, sliced
- 1½ oz. boursin cheese

Instructions:

1. Cut the cucumber in half, then use a spoon to remove the seeds and core. With caution, remove the tough outer layer using a knife.

2. Arrange the cheese on one side. On the other side, fold the meat. Combine to create a sandwich!

Nutritional Information:

Calories: 195

Net Carbs: 8g

Fat: 14g

Protein: 18g

Chili Soup

Serves: 8

Ingredients:

- 2 tbsp. butter, unsalted
- 1 tbsp. coconut flour
- 2 onions
- 8 chicken thighs (boneless)
- 1 pepper
- 8 slices of bacon
- 1 tsp. thyme
- 1 tsp. salt
- 1 tsp. pepper
- 1 tbsp. garlic, minced
- 1 cup chicken stock

- 3 tbsp. tomato paste
- ¼ cup unsweetened coconut milk
- 3 tbsp. lemon juice

Instructions:

1. Place the butter in the middle of the Crock-Pot.

2. Add the pepper and onion slices to the Crock-Pot. After that, add the chicken thighs. Place the slices of bacon on top.

3. Add coconut flour, minced garlic, salt, and pepper for seasoning. Incorporate the tomato paste, coconut milk, chicken stocks, and lemon juice.

4. Simmer on low for six hours. When cooked, give it a toss and serve.

Nutritional Information:

Calories: 395

Net Carbs: 8g

Fat: 20g

Protein: 40g

Cauliflower Rice With Chicken

Serves: 6

Ingredients:

- 4 chicken breasts
- 1 cup water
- 1 packet curry paste
- 3 tbsp. ghee
- 1 head cauliflower
- ½ cup heavy cream

Instructions:

1. Melt the ghee in a big pan, then add the curry and stir. After mixing well, pour in the water and simmer for five minutes.

2. Cook the chicken for an additional 20 minutes with a lid on. Add the cream and cook for an extra five minutes when it's finished.

3. Separately make the cauliflower rice by chopping and shredding the head into florets. In a frying pan, sauté some butter or olive oil, then reduce the heat to low and cover. Steam for five to eight minutes.

4. Serve with the curry chicken.

Nutritional Information:

Calories: 350

Net Carbs: 10g

Fat: 16g

Protein: 40g

Chicken Nuggets For Keto Nuts

Serves: 4

Ingredients:

- 1 chicken breast, precooked
- 2 tbsp. almond flour
- ½ ounce grated parmesan
- ½ tsp. baking powder
- 1 tbsp. water
- 1 egg

Instructions:

1. After slicing the chicken breast, chop it into bite-sized pieces. Put aside.

2. Mix the water, baking powder, almond flour, and parmesan. Stir.

3. After dipping the chicken pieces into the batter, drop them straight into the boiling oil. When golden, remove.

Nutritional Information:

Calories: 165

Net Carbs: 3g

Fat: 9g

Protein: 25g

Zucchini Keto Wraps

Serves: 6

Ingredients:

- 1 zucchini
- Salt and pepper
- 1 tbsp. dried mint
- 6 oz. soft goat's cheese
- Oil
- 1 tsp. dried dill

Instructions:

1. Slice off the zucchini's ends. Cut into ⅛-inch pieces and drizzle with olive oil. Cook the outside and the inside.

2. Blend the dill, mint, and goat's cheese together. Cut it into six pieces.

3. Use a toothpick to attach the zucchini slices around the cheese bits.

Nutritional Information:

Calories: 188

Net Carbs: 4g

Fat: 14g

Protein: 15g

Keto Casserole With Chicken And Bacon

Serves: 12

Ingredients:

- 12 chicken thighs
- 16 oz. frozen cauliflower
- 1 small onion
- 24 oz. Jimmy Dean sausage
- 4 celery stalks

- 16 oz. sliced mushrooms
- 7 slices bacon
- 8 oz. shredded cheddar cheese
- Paprika
- 16 oz. cream cheese, softened

Instructions:

1. Bake the bacon for fifteen minutes at 400°F.

2. In the interim, dice the chicken and sear it in a frying skillet. Take it out of the pan.

3. The sausage should be browned. When finished, put it in the same bowl with the chicken.

4. Chop the celery and onion and sauté them in the leftover sausage oil until they become transparent.

5. After defrosting, chop the cauliflower florets into smaller pieces.

6. Combine all the ingredients in a big bowl and thoroughly stir. Stir in the cream cheese thoroughly.

7. Transfer the mixture to a large pan and top with the paprika.

8. Bake, covered with foil, for 30 minutes at 350°F. After 10 more minutes, uncover and continue cooking.

Nutritional Information:

Calories: 600

Net Carbs: 6g

Fat: 41g

Protein: 53g

Cauliflower Soup With Bacon And Cheddar

Serves: 6

Ingredients:

- 1 head of cauliflower
- ¼ cup heavy cream
- tbsp. olive oil
- 1 medium onion, diced
- 1 tbsp. minced garlic
- 4 slices bacon
- 1 tsp. thyme
- 12 oz. aged cheddar
- 3 cups chicken broth

- 1 oz. parmesan cheese

Instructions:

1. After chopping, put the cauliflower on a baking pan covered with foil. For seasoning, add a little olive oil, salt, and pepper. Bake at 375°F for 35 minutes.

2. Cook the bacon in a pot until it's crispy. After adding the chopped onion, fry it in bacon grease. Add the garlic and thyme once it's soft, and simmer for a minute or so.

3. Add the cauliflower and chicken broth, then cook for 20 minutes with a lid on.

4. When the allotted time has passed, puree the ingredients in a food processor or blender. Reassemble the pot. Incorporate the cheddar and parmesan cheeses, stirring until they melt.

5. Lastly, thoroughly whisk in the bacon and double cream. Simmer for a further 10 minutes, or until warm, if necessary.

Nutritional Information:

Calories: 340

Net Carbs: 10g

Fat: 26g

Protein: 20g

Mexican-Style Casserole With Spinach

Serves: 12

Ingredients:

- 1 onion
- 1 green pepper
- 20 oz. drained spinach
- 2 cans drained diced tomatoes with green chilies
- 2 lb. ground pork
- 10 tbsp. sour cream
- 16 oz. cream cheese
- 8 oz. mozzarella cheese, shredded
- Jalapeños, sliced
- 4 tsp. taco seasoning

Instructions:

1. Cook the chopped onion and pepper until they become transparent. Add diced jalapeños if desired.

2. Transfer the onion and pepper to a basin.

3. Add a little olive oil to a frying pan and wilt the spinach to cook. Once it's finished, transfer it to the bowl.

4. Cook the ground pork and brown it. Use taco seasoning to season.

5. Add the sour cream, mozzarella, and cream cheese to the bowl along with the diced tomato. Transfer the blend onto a baking dish and cook it for 40 minutes at 350°F.

Nutritional Information:

Calories: 400

Net Carbs: 10g

Fat: 30g

Protein: 25g

Chicken Salad

Serves: 6

Ingredients:

- 4 chicken breasts
- 4½ oz. celery
- 4 oz. green peppers
- 1½ cups cream
- 1 ounce green onions
- ¾ cup mayo
- ¾ cup sugar free sweet relish
- eggs, hard-boiled

Instructions:

1. Place the chicken in an ovenproof pan and top with cream. Cook at 350°F for 40–60 minutes. Once finished, allow it to cool. Throw away the liquid.

2. Add the chopped onions, pepper, and celery to a bowl. Add the chicken after it's diced.

3. Gently stir in the chopped, hard-boiled eggs.

3. Split into six separate containers.

Nutritional Information:

Calories: 415

Net Carbs: 4g

Fat: 24g

Protein: 40g

Almond Pizza

Serves: 4

Ingredients:

- 1½ tsp. baking powder
- ¾ cup almond meal
- 1½ tsp. granulated sweetener
- ½ tsp. oregano
- ¼ tsp. thyme
- 2 eggs
- ½ tsp. garlic powder
- 5 tbsp. butter
- 4 oz. cheddar cheese
- ½ cup alfredo sauce

Instructions:

1. In a large bowl, mix together the dry ingredients.

2. Add the eggs to the dry ingredients once they are at room temperature.

3. Add the melted butter and mix.

4. Spread the crust out on a pizza pan coated with oil, and bake it for about 7 minutes at 350°F.

5. Take it out of the oven and cover it with cheddar cheese and Alfredo sauce. Cook for a further five minutes.

Nutritional Information:

Calories: 460

Net Carbs: 5g

Fat: 45g

Protein: 15g

Keto Chicken Thighs

Serves: 6

Ingredients:

- 16 chicken thighs (boneless skinless)
- 8 oz. cheddar cheese, shredded
- 2 cups water
- 24 oz. spinach
- Garlic powder

- Salt and pepper

Instructions:

1. Bake the chicken thighs for 20 minutes at 350°F in a covered skillet with two cups of water. Take it out and allow it to cool.

2. Add the cheese, spinach, and seasonings after breaking the chicken into pieces.

Nutritional Information:

Calories: 390

Net Carbs: 4g

Fat: 25g

Protein: 47g

Keto Pork Stew

Serves: 4

Ingredients:

- 1 lb. pork shoulder, cooked and sliced
- 2 tsp. cumin
- 2 tsp. chili powder

- 1 tsp. garlic, minced
- ½ tsp. pepper
- ½ tsp. salt
- 1 tsp. paprika
- 1 tsp. oregano
- 2 bay leaves
- 6 oz. button mushrooms
- ¼ tsp. cinnamon
- ½ jalapeño, sliced
- ½ onion, medium
- ½ sliced green bell pepper
- ½ sliced red bell pepper
- 2 cups gelatinous bone broth
- Juice of ½ a lime
- 2 cups chicken broth
- ½ cup strong coffee
- ¼ cup tomato paste

Instructions:

1. Cut up the veggies and cook them on high heat in a pan coated with olive oil. Once browned, remove from heat.

2. Add the chopped pork, mushrooms, chicken broth, bone broth, and coffee to a slow cooker.

3. Add the vegetables and seasonings to the mixture. Put the cover on. Cook on low for 4–10 hours.

Nutritional Information:

Calories: 385

Net Carbs: 6.4g

Fat: 29g

Protein: 20g

Bbq Chicken Soup

Serves:4

Ingredients:

- 3 medium chicken thighs
- 2 tbsp. olive oil
- 2 tsp. chili seasoning
- 1½ cups chicken broth
- ¼ cup reduced sugar ketchup
- 1½ cups beef broth BBQ sauce
- ¼ cup tomato paste
- 1 tbsp. soy sauce
- tbsp. Dijon mustard
- 2½ tsp. liquid smoke
- 1 tbsp. hot sauce

- 1½ tsp. garlic powder
- 1 tsp. Worcestershire sauce
- 1 tsp. chili powder
- 1 tsp. onion powder
- 1 tsp. red chili flakes
- ¼ cup butter
- 1 tsp. cumin
- Salt and pepper

Instructions:

1. Remove the bones from the chicken thighs. Keep the bones aside. Add your preferred chili spices and seasoning. Place on a foil-lined baking sheet and bake for 50 minutes at 400°F.

2. Heat the olive oil in a pot over medium-high heat. Add the chicken bones once they've heated through. After 5 minutes of cooking, add the broth. Add pepper and salt for seasoning.

3. Remove the chicken's skin when it's done. Add the rendered chicken fat to the broth and stir.

4. To make the BBQ sauce, mix together all of the ingredients listed above. After adding it to the pot, stir. Give it a 20–30 minute simmer.

5. Using an immersion blender, emulsify all the liquids and fats together. Add the chicken shreds to the soup and stir. Cook for a further 10 to 20 minutes.

Nutritional Information:

Calories: 490

Net Carbs: 4.5g

Fat: 38g

Protein: 25g

Keto Enchilada Soup

Serves: 4

Ingredients:

- 3 tbsp. olive oil
- 1 medium diced red bell pepper
- 3 diced celery stalks
- 2 tsp. minced garlic
- 1 cup diced tomatoes
- 1 tsp. oregano

- 2 tsp. cumin
- 1 tsp. chili powder
- ½ cup chopped cilantro
- ½ tsp. cayenne pepper
- cups chicken broth
- 6 oz. shredded chicken
- 8 oz. cream cheese
- Juice of ½ a lime

Instructions:

1. In a heated pan, add the pepper and celery and sauté them with olive oil. Add the tomatoes and simmer for an additional two to three minutes after the celery begins to soften.

2. Stir in the spices. Bring the chicken stock to a boil after adding the cilantro. After lowering the heat to low, simmer for roughly 20 minutes.

3. Add the cheese and re-boil. Simmer for a further twenty-five minutes on low heat.

4. Stir in the lime juice and chicken shreds. Stir.

5. Add some cilantro for seasoning, and serve.

Nutritional Information:

Calories: 345

Net Carbs: 6.3g

Fat: 31g

Protein: 13g

Keto Caprese Salad

Serves: 2.

Ingredients:

- 1 Tomato
- ¼ cup chopped fresh basil
- 6 oz. fresh mozzarella cheese
- Freshly cracked black pepper
- 3 tbsp. olive oil
- Salt

Instructions:

1. In a food processor, add a little oil and fresh basil. Mix until a paste is formed.

2. Chop the mozzarella and cut the tomatoes. Place a layer of mozzarella and basil paste on top of each tomato. Salt, black pepper, and olive oil are used to season.

Nutritional Information:

Calories: 407

Net Carbs: 3.7g

Fat: 38g

Protein: 16g

Grilled Cheese Sandwich
Serves: 1.

Ingredients:

- 2 eggs
- 2 tbsp. almond flour
- 1½ tbsp. psyllium husk powder
- ½ tsp. baking powder
- 2 oz. cheddar cheese
- 2 tbsp. soft butter
- 1 tbsp. butter

Instructions:

1. To make the bun, combine the eggs, butter, almond flour, psyllium husk powder, and baking powder. It needs to be really thick. Transfer the mixture to a square container and let it settle until it levels out. For ninety seconds, microwave.

2. Once done, take it out and cut it in half. Sandwich the cheese between the buns, and cook in a skillet over medium heat with melted butter.

Nutritional Information:

Calories: 794

Net Carbs: 5g

Fat: 72g

Protein: 30g

Vegetarian Curry

Serves: 2.

Ingredients:

- 4 tbsp. coconut oil
- 1 cup broccoli florets Spinach
- tsp. garlic, minced
- 1 tbsp. red curry paste
- tsp. fish sauce
- ½ cup coconut cream (or coconut milk)
- 1 tsp. ginger
- 2 tsp. soy sauce
- ¼ onion, chopped

Instructions:

1. Place a pan with the coconut oil over medium-high heat. Once heated, sauté the onions until they turn golden. Include the garlic. Add the broccoli and reduce the heat to medium-low. Stir.

2. Add the curry paste to the broccoli when it is half cooked. Give it one minute to cook.

3. Include the spinach. Add the coconut oil and cream once it's cooked.

3. Stir in the fish sauce, ginger, and soy sauce. Simmer for ten minutes or so.

Nutritional Information:

Calories: 395

Net Carbs: 7g

Fat: 40g

Protein: 6g

Asian Salad

Serves: 1.

Ingredients:

- 2 tbsp. coconut oil
- 1 packet shirataki noodles
- 1 cucumber
- 1 spring onion
- 1 tbsp. sesame oil
- ¼ tbsp. red pepper flakes
- 1 tbsp. rice vinegar
- 1 tsp. sesame seeds
- Salt and pepper

Instructions:

1. Clean the shirataki-made noodles. Straining removes all of the excess water. Let them dry on paper towels.

2. Heat the coconut oil in a pan over medium-high heat and cook the noodles

for five to seven minutes. To cool, remove it and place it on a paper towel.

3. Slice and peel the cucumber. Place on a platter, then top with the remaining ingredients, scattering them over the cucumber. Chill in the refrigerator for thirty minutes.

4. Add fried shirataki noodles as topping.

Nutritional Information:

Calories: 418

Net Carbs: 8g

Protein: 3g

Fat: 45g

DINNER RECIPES
Noodles & glazed salmon

Serves 4

Prep time: 5 minutes

Cook time: 20 minutes

Ingredients:

- 1/4 cup plus 2 tablespoons (75 ml) avocado oil, divided
- teaspoon sesame seeds
- 4 cloves garlic, minced
- ½ teaspoon finely ground sea salt
- tablespoons plus 2 teaspoons tomato paste
- ¼ cup (60 ml) coconut aminos
- green onions, sliced
- A handful of fresh cilantro leaves, roughly chopped
- 2 tablespoons apple cider vinegar
- 1 (2-in/5-cm) piece fresh ginger root, grated
- 1 pound (455 g) salmon fillets, cut into 4 equal portions

- 2 (7-oz/198-g) packages konjac noodles or equivalent amount of other low-carb noodles of choice

Instructions:

1. In a large frying pan over medium heat, add two teaspoons of oil.

2. Make the sauce while the oil is still heating up. In a small bowl, mix the remaining ¼ cup of oil, salt, coconut aminos, tomato paste, ginger, vinegar, and garlic.

3. The salmon should be placed in the heated pan, the heat should be reduced, and the sauce should be applied. Drizzle any remaining sauce into the skillet. Once sealed, simmer over low heat for about 15 minutes, or until it starts to sear and slightly cook.

4. When the salmon is cooked, place it heapingly on the pan's side, giving the noodles plenty of space. In the pan, toss in the noodles and green onions to combine with the remaining sauce. Place the cooked salmon on top of the noodles. Cook for a further three to five

minutes, or until the noodles are heated through.

5. Pour the cilantro and sesame seeds over the salmon. Divide the noodles and salmon among four dinner plates, then drizzle the leftover pan sauce over each dish. enjoy the dish.

Nutritional Information:

Calories: 333

Protein:30%

Fat:61%

Carbs:10%

Crispy thighs & mash

Serves 6

Prep time: 15 minutes

Cook time: 30 minutes

Ingredients:

CRISPY CHICKEN:

- ½ teaspoon onion powder

- ¼ teaspoon ground black pepper
- 6 small or 3 large boneless, skinless chicken thighs (about 1 lb/455 g)
- ¼ teaspoon finely ground sea salt
- ¼ cup (60 ml) melted coconut oil or avocado oil
- teaspoon garlic powder

MASH WITH BUTTERNUT:

- 1½ tablespoons chicken bone broth
- ⅓ cup (80 ml) milk (nondairy or regular)
- medium butternut squash (about 1¼ lbs/570 g)
- tablespoons coconut oil or ghee
- ½ teaspoon finely ground sea salt
- ⅛ teaspoon ground black pepper

Instructions:

1. Cook chicken well enough: Set the oven temperature to 400°F, or roughly 205°C. If you wish to use large chicken thigh, they can be used by slicing them in half to yield six pieces. Transfer the chicken to a rimmed baking sheet. Cover the thighs with oil and mist them

with spices. By stirring the thighs, coat them thoroughly in the oil and spices. Bake the chicken for 25 to 30 minutes, or until the internal temperature reaches 165°F (74°C). Thinly slice the chicken into ½-inch pieces.

2. In the meantime, prepare the mash by removing the cover, seeding it, and slicing the flesh into pieces. Measure out the 3 cups (455 g) of squash cubes that you'll need for the mash; save any leftovers in the fridge for later.

3. Over medium heat, warm the oil in a large frying pan. Add the squash, pepper, and salt. After covering and cooking for ten to fifteen minutes, the squash should start to brown. After adding the milk and broth, cover the pan and simmer the squash for a further 15 minutes, or until it is fork-tender. When the squash is ready, use the back of a fork to mash it right in the pan.

4. For serving, split the mash between six dishes. Use an equal amount of sliced chicken as toppings.

5. Enjoy your meal.

Nutritional information:

calories: 331

Fat: 70%

Protein: 19%

Carbs: 11%

Scallops & Mozza broccoli mash

Serves 4

Prep time: 5 minutes

Cook time: 35 minutes

Ingredients:

MOZZA BROCCOLI MASH:

- 4 cloves garlic, minced
- ⅔ cup (160 ml) chicken bone broth
- ¼ cup (55 g) coconut oil or ghee, or ¼ cup (60 ml) avocado oil
- 6 cups (570 g) broccoli florets

- (2-in/5-cm) piece fresh ginger root, grated
- ½ cup (70 g) shredded mozzarella cheese (dairy-free or regular)

SCALLOPS:

- Lemon wedges
- ¼ teaspoon finely ground sea salt
- pound (455 g) sea scallops
- ¼ teaspoon ground black pepper
- tablespoons coconut oil, avocado oil, or ghee

Instructions:

1. To prepare the mash, heat the oil in a large saucepan over low heat. Ginger, garlic, and broccoli should all be added. Cook uncovered for five minutes or so, or until the garlic becomes fragrant.

2. When the broccoli mashes easily, simmer on medium-low heat for 25 minutes after adding the broth, sealing the pot.

3. Prepare the scallops five minutes before the broccoli is ready. Dry them off, and sprinkle salt and pepper on both

sides of the scallops. In a medium-sized frying pan over medium heat, warm the oil. When the oil is heated, add the scallops. Cook until golden, about 2 minutes per side.

4. When the broccoli is done, add the cheese and use a fork to mash it. Arrange the mash on four plates, then top with the scallops. Accompany with wedges of lemon, and enjoy!

Nutritional Information:

Calories: 353

Protein:22%

Fat:65%

Carbs:14%

Cream of mushroom–stuffed chicken

Serves 4

Prep time: 10 minutes

Cook time: 45 minutes

Ingredients:

- 1 teaspoon garlic powder
- 3 tablespoons coconut oil, avocado oil, or ghee
- 7 ounces (200 g) cremini mushrooms, chopped
- 4 cloves garlic, minced
- 1 teaspoon onion powder
- ¼ teaspoon ground black pepper
- teaspoons dried parsley, divided
- ¾ teaspoon finely ground sea salt, divided
- 4 cups (280 g) spinach, for serving
- 1 pound (455 g) boneless, skin-on chicken breasts
- ½ cup (120 ml) milk (nondairy or regular)

Instructions:

1. Turn the oven on to 400°F. Arrange the silicone baking mat or parchment paper on a rimmed baking pan.

2. In a large saucepan over medium heat, heat the oil. Add the garlic, pepper, ¼ teaspoon of salt, two teaspoons of parsley, and mushrooms. After tossing, allow to coat and cook for approximately ten minutes.

3. While waiting, cut each chicken breast horizontally, stopping the knife about ½ inch (1.25 cm) from the other side so it may open wide (like a book); be careful not to cut through the breasts. Using a sharp knife and supporting the breast with your palm can help you maintain its stability. This is the best method for doing this.

4. The chicken breasts should be placed on the lined baking sheet and then opened. In the center of each open breast, place ¼ of the mushroom mixture. If any mushroom mixture is left, add it to the pan and cover the chicken.

5. Fold over the chicken breasts to reveal the stuffing. Season the stuffed breasts with the last ½ teaspoon of salt,

onion powder, garlic powder, and one teaspoon of parsley.

6. Fill the space between the chicken breasts in the pan straight.

7. Bake until the chicken reaches an internal temperature of 165°F, which should take 30 to 35 minutes.

8. Divide the spinach between four dinner plates. Divide the filled chicken breasts among the plates, dress the spinach with the velvety pan jus, and enjoy!

Nutritional Information:

Calories: 388

Protein:38%

Fat:55%

Carbs:7%

Bbq beef & slaw

Serves 4

Prep time: 10 minutes

Cook time: 45 minutes or 4 to 6 hours(depends on the method)

Ingredients:

BBQ BEEF:

- ½ cup (80 g) sugar-free barbecue sauce
- cup (240 ml) beef bone broth
- pound (455 g) boneless beef chuck roast
- ½ teaspoon finely ground sea salt

SLAW:

- ½ cup (120 ml) sugar-free poppy seed dressing
- 9 ounces (255 g) coleslaw mix

Instructions:

1. Add the stock, chuck roast, and salt. To use a pressure cooker, place it on high pressure and cook for around 45 minutes while covered. After finishing, wait for the pressure to subside before removing the lid naturally. Cook for approximately four hours on high pressure and six hours on low heat if you're using a slow cooker.

2. When the meat is done, drain the liquid completely, leaving about ¼ cup of liquid in the cooker. Toss to coat the beef after adding the barbecue sauce and shredding it with two forks.

3. To coat, place the coleslaw dressing mixture in a salad bowl and toss.

4. Divide the barbecued beef and coleslaw among four plates; top with the slaw after the steak is cooked, enjoy.

Nutritional Information:

Calories: 354

Protein:27%

Fat:68%

Carbs:5%

Crispy pork with lemon-thyme cauli rice

Serves 4

Prep time: 5 minutes

Cook time: 40 minutes

Ingredients:

CRISPY PORK:

¼ teaspoon ground black pepper

¼ cup (55 g) coconut oil or ghee, or ¼ cup (60 ml) avocado oil

½ teaspoon finely ground sea salt

½ cup (38 g) crushed pork rinds

1 teaspoon dried thyme leaves

1 teaspoon garlic powder

1 pound (455 g) boneless pork chops (about 1 in/2.5 cm thick)

1 teaspoon dried oregano leaves

LEMON-THYME CAULI RICE:

- 1 medium head cauliflower (about 1½ lbs/680 g), or 3 cups (375 g) pre-riced cauliflower
- 1 small white onion, diced
- Leaves from 6 sprigs fresh thyme
- ¼ cup (60 ml) chicken bone broth
- ½ tablespoons lemon juice
- ½ teaspoon finely ground sea salt

- cloves garlic, minced

Instructions:

1. In a large saucepan over medium-low heat, heat the oil.

2. While the oil is still heating, add the salt, pepper, garlic powder, oregano and thyme in a medium-sized bowl. Once blended, add the pork chops one at a time, stirring to coat each one. Once the chops are well coated, transfer the mixture to a saucepan.

3. Sear the pork chops for about ten minutes on each side, or until well done.

4. Move on to Step 5 if you are using pre-riced cauliflower. If not, cut off the cauliflower's bottom and remove the florets. To chop the florets into tiny pieces, transfer them to a blender and pulse three to four times.

5. After the pork has cooked for approximately 20 minutes, transfer the chops to a platter, leaving the cooking oil in the pan. Add the broth, riced

cauliflower, onion, garlic, lemon juice, and salt. Cook the cauliflower rice, covered, for about 15 minutes, stirring periodically, until it becomes tender.

6. Meanwhile, cut the pork chops into pieces that are ½ inch thick. In a skillet of cooked cauliflower rice, add the sliced pork. Cook the pork for a further five minutes, uncovered, if it's still not cooked through.

7. Split the pork and cauliflower rice among four dishes, then scatter the thyme leaves over top. Enjoy yourself!

Nutritional information:

Calories: 419

Protein:34%

Fat:58%

Carbs:8%

Salmon & kale

Serves 4

Prep time: 5 minutes, plus 2 hours to marinate

Cook time: 15 minutes

Ingredients:

- ¼ teaspoon finely ground sea salt
- 1 pound (455 g) salmon fillets
- ¾ cup (180 ml) vinaigrette of choice
- 1 small red onion, sliced
- 4 cups (240 g) destemmed kale leaves
- ¼ teaspoon red pepper flakes

Instructions:

1. Pour the vinaigrette over the salmon after placing it in a shallow dish. To marinate for 120 minutes, cover and keep in the fridge.

2. When you're ready to cook, transfer the salmon to a large frying pan, along with the marinade. Turn the heat down to medium, and cover the fish with onion pieces. Sear the salmon for six minutes on each side, cooking it continuously.

3. After cooking for around 12 minutes, move the salmon to the side of the pan so that the kale can go there. Toss to coat the greens with the pan drippings after adding the salt, red pepper flakes, and kale. Once the kale has wilted, cover and cook for around three minutes.

4. Serve the salmon fillets and braised greens on four separate plates.

Nutritional Information:

Calories: 438

Carbs:8%

Fat:68%

Protein:24%

One-pot porky kale

Serves 4

Prep time: 5 minutes

Cook time: 35 minutes

Ingredients:

- ¼ cup (17 g) chopped fresh parsley
- 3 tablespoons coconut oil, avocado oil, or ghee
- 4 cups (240 g) destemmed kale leaves
- 1 teaspoon paprika
- ½ teaspoon finely ground sea salt
- ¼ teaspoon ground black pepper
- 1 small yellow onion, sliced
- ⅓ cup (80 ml) creamy Italian dressing
- 6 cloves garlic, minced
- 1 pound (455 g) boneless pork chops (about 1 in/2.5 cm thick)

Instructions:

1. Heat the oil in a large skillet over medium heat.

2. Put the salt, pepper, and paprika in a medium-sized bowl and set aside while the oil heats. Blend well, then add the pork chops one at a time, coating each one with the paprika mixture after mixing.

3. The coated pork chops should sear thoroughly after 10 minutes of cooking on each side.

4. After about 20 minutes of cooking, remove the chops from the pan and place them on a clean plate. After adding the garlic and onion, simmer for five minutes, or until aromatic.

5. After adding the dressing and kale to the pan, heat it continuously for two minutes, watching out that the kale doesn't wilt. Take it out of the heat.

6. Cut the pork chops into halves or quarters. In order to ensure that the meat is cooked through, place the slices in the pan and cook them uncovered for an additional five minutes.

7. Share over 4 dishes, topped with parsley, and enjoy!

Nutritional information:

Calories: 429

Fat:65%

Protein: 26%

Carbs: 9%

Creamy spinach zucchini boats

Makes 8 boats (2 per serving)

Prep time: 15 minutes

Cook time: 30 minutes

Ingredients:

- 4 medium zucchinis
- 1 cup (250 g) coconut cream
- 1 packed cup (70 g) spinach, finely chopped
- ¼ teaspoon red pepper flakes
- ½ cup (105 g) mayonnaise
- ⅓ cup (55 g) collagen peptides (optional)
- ¼ teaspoon paprika
- 1 tablespoon onion powder
- 2 teaspoons garlic powder
- ½ teaspoon finely ground sea salt
- 1¼ cups (95 g) crushed pork rinds

Instructions:

1. Warm the oven up to roughly 400°F. Line a 13 x 9" baking pan with parchment paper for simple cleanup.

2. In order to avoid breaking the zucchini in half, cut them in half lengthwise, making sure the stems remain whole. Then, using a spoon, remove the insides, leaving the margins at least ¼ to ½ inch thick.

3. Fill the lined baking pan with the emptied-out zucchini, edge-up.

4. Transfer the remaining ingredients, excluding the pork rinds, to a blender and process until smooth. Finally, hand-stirring the spinach to incorporate it.

5. Serve the spinach solution fully filled with the aid of a spoon into the zucchini boats, then top the boats with a mound of crumbled pork rinds.

6. Bake for thirty minutes, or until the tops are lightly golden, then leave it to cool for ten minutes before serving.

Nutritional Information:

Calories: 453

Carbs: 8%

Fat: 64%

Protein: 28%

Original Keto Burger with Portobello Bun

Serves: 1

Ingredients:

- 1 garlic clove
- ½ tbsp. organic extra virgin coconut oil
- 1 tbsp. oregano
- 1 tbsp. Dijon mustard
- 6 oz. organic grass fed beef or bison
- 2 Portobello mushroom caps
- 1 tsp. salt
- ¼ cup cheddar cheese Salt and pepper
- 1 tsp. freshly ground black pepper

Instructions:

1. Cut off the gills and stems from the Portobello mushrooms.

2. Coconut oil, garlic, oregano, salt, and pepper should all be combined in a basin. As you finish the other procedures, marinate the portobello mushrooms in the mixture.

3. The ground meat, mustard, salt, black pepper, and cheddar cheese should all be combined in a different bowl. Shape the patties.

4. Grill the mushroom tops for seven to ten minutes. Burgers should be taken out and cooked for six minutes on each side.

5. Take both out of the oven and put the burger together. After adding your chosen toppings, serve.

Nutritional information:

Calories: 730

Net Carbs: 5g

Fat: 50g

Protein: 60g

My favourite creamy pesto chicken

Serves 4

Prep time: 10 minutes

Cook time: 20 minutes

Ingredients:

CHICKEN:

- ¼ cup (60 ml) avocado oil
- ⅛ teaspoon red pepper flakes
- ½ teaspoon dried thyme leaves
- 1 pound (455 g) boneless, skinless chicken breasts, thinly sliced
- 1 small white onion, thinly sliced
- ¾ teaspoon dried oregano leaves
- ½ cup (105 g) sun-dried tomatoes, drained and chopped

PESTO CREAM SAUCE:

- ½ teaspoon ground black pepper
- 2 cloves garlic
- ¼ cup (37 g) pine nuts
- ¼ cup (17 g) nutritional yeast
- ½ cup (120 ml) chicken bone broth
- ½ teaspoon finely ground sea salt
- ½ cup (120 ml) full-fat coconut milk

- ½ ounce (14 g) fresh basil leaves and stems
- 2 medium zucchinis, spiral sliced, raw or cooked, for serving

Instructions:

1. Heat the oil in a large skillet over medium heat. Add the chicken, thyme, onion, oregano, sun-dried tomatoes, and red pepper flakes. Sauté for approximately five minutes, or until aromatic.

2. While waiting for the sauce to turn green (bright), add all the ingredients for the pesto cream sauce to a blender and process on high until smooth, about 30 seconds. Then add the basil and pulse to split it up a little, but don't pulse the basil until the sauce turns green.

3. Pour the sauce into the pan and mix to coat the chicken. Reduce the heat to low, cover, and simmer for about 15 minutes, stirring occasionally, until the chicken is cooked through.

4. Split the sliced zucchini into four equal portions for dinner, then top each with a corresponding quantity of chicken and sauce.

Nutritional information:

Calories: 455

Carbs: 14%

Fat: 58%

Protein: 28%

Keto Pork Chops

Serves: 4

Ingredients:

- ½ tsp. peppercorns
- 1 stalk lemongrass
- 1 medium star anise
- 4 halved garlic cloves
- 4 pork chops (boneless)
- 1 tbsp. almond flour
- 1 tbsp. fish sauce
- 1½ tsp. soy sauce
- ½ tsp. five spice

- 1 tsp. sesame oil
- ½ tbsp. sugar free ketchup
- ½ tbsp. sambal chili paste

Instructions:

1. Grind the star anise and peppercorns (in a mortar or blender).

2. Combine the lemongrass with the garlic, five spice powders, fish sauce, soy sauce, and sesame oil. Stir in the star anise and peppercorn powder. In a food processor, blend until well blended.

3. Place the pork on a tray and generously coat both sides with the mixture. Marinate for one to two hours with the tray covered.

4. Dredge each pork chop in a little amount of almond flour and cook it on high heat. Sear the outside. Ensure that they are completed on both sides.

5. Take out and cut into strips.

6. To make the dipping sauce, combine the sugar-free ketchup and sambal chili paste, then serve.

Nutritional Information:

Calories: 224

Net Carbs: 5g

Fat: 10g

Protein: 35g

Pork Hock

Serves: 2.

Ingredients:

- 1 lb. pork hock
- 1 tsp. oregano
- ¼ cup rice vinegar
- ⅓ cup shaoxing cooking wine
- ⅓ cup soy sauce
- ¼ cup sweetener
- 1 tbsp. butter Shiitake mushrooms
- ⅓ onion
- 1 tsp. Chinese five-spice
- 2 crushed garlic cloves

Instructions:

1. In a frying pan, cook the onions until they become semi-transparent. In the interim, bring the mushrooms to a soft boil.

2. Sear the pork hock in a third pan until it's browned all over.

3. Add all the ingredients to a Crockpot and simmer on high heat for two hours after a few minutes. Cook for an additional two hours after stirring.

4. Once the pork has been removed, bone it. Cut it into slices and return it to the saucepan to absorb flavors.

5. Serve the dish alongside the vegetables.

Nutritional Information:

Calories: 550

Net Carbs: 20g

Fat: 32g

Protein: 50g

Meatballs With Bacon And Cheese

Serves: 5.

Ingredients:

Instructions:

1. Process the pig rinds for it to create a powder.

2. Combine the ground beef, garlic powder, cumin, pig rinds, and salt and pepper. Completely incorporate the cheese.

3. Slice the bacon thinly and cook it in a hot skillet until it's the right consistency. Give them time to cool. Mix the bacon thoroughly with the meat.

4. Shape the meatballs.

3. After browning the meatballs on both sides, cook them in a pan and cover with a lid for ten minutes. After they're done, let them sit for about five minutes before eating. Add your chosen sauce over top.

Nutritional Information:

Calories: 450

Net Carbs: 3g

Fat: 26g

Protein: 50g

Keto Crisp Pizza

Serves: 12

Ingredients:

- 8 oz. package of cream cheese (at room temperature)
- 1 tsp. garlic powder
- ¼ cup parmesan cheese, grated 2 eggs
- ½ lb. ground beef
- ½ tsp. cumin
- 1 chorizo sausage
- ¼ tsp. basil
- ¼ tsp. turmeric
- ½ tsp. Italian seasoning
- Salt and pepper

Instructions:

1. Using a hand mixer, combine cream cheese, parmesan cheese, eggs, pepper, and garlic.

2. Apply butter grease to a baking pan. Evenly distribute the dough mixture inside. Cook at 375°F for 12 to 15 minutes in the oven.

3. In a frying pan, cook the meat and then add the spices turmeric, cumin, basil, and Italian seasoning.

4. After the pizza dough is finished, let it cool for ten minutes before adding some cheese and tomato sauce on top. After baking for an additional 10 minutes, add the meat as the cheese begins to melt. Five more minutes of boiling. Once cooked, allow it to cool before slicing.

Nutritional Information:

Calories: 145

Net Carbs: 1g

Fat: 12g

Protein: 9g

Bacon Wrapped Chicken

Serves: 4

Ingredients:

- 2 skinless chicken breasts, boneless
- 4 slices ham
- 4 oz. blue cheese
- 8 slices bacon

Instructions:

1. Cut the breasts in half along their length.

2. Arrange a pair of ham slices with a line of cheese positioned in the center. After rolling the chicken breast, place it inside.

3. Four bacon pieces should completely round the chicken breast.

4. After greasing the skillet with butter or coconut oil, place the breasts inside and cook the bacon until it's browned all over. Take out of the skillet and transfer to a 325°F oven for 45 minutes. Before serving, let it settle for ten minutes.

Nutritional Information:

Calories: 270

Net Carbs: 0.50g

Fat: 11g

Protein: 38g

Little Portobello Pizza

Serves: 1.

Ingredients:

- 3 Portobello mushrooms
- 3 tomato slices
- Olive oil
- 9 spinach leaves
- 3 tsp. pizza seasoning
- 1½ oz. Monterey jack
- 1½ oz. mozzarella
- 12 pepperoni slices
- 1½ oz. cheddar cheese

Instructions:

1. Wash and trim the Portobello mushrooms, making sure to remove the stems and gills.

2. After sprinkling with pizza seasoning and olive oil, top with all the remaining

ingredients, excluding the pepperoni pieces.

3. Simmer for 6 minutes at 450°F. When the pepperoni slices are crispy, add them and broil.

Nutritional Information:

Calories: 275

Net Carbs: 5g

Fat: 20g

Protein: 20g

Keto Broccoli Soup

Serves: 4

Ingredients:

- 1 head broccoli
- ¼ cup cream cheese
- ¼ cup heavy cream
- ¼ cup sour cream
- ½ onion
- 4 oz. cheddar cheese
- ¼ cup almond milk
- ½ chicken bouillon cube

Instructions

1. Take out the broccoli's florets. Put them on the stove to steam.

2. Place the cauliflower florets in a blender along with the remaining ingredients. Blend the mixture until the appropriate consistency is achieved.

3. Pour into a pot and let it simmer for around ten minutes to get cooked.

Nutritional Information:

Calories: 270

Net Carbs: 8g

Fat: 25g

Protein: 10g

Cheddar Biscuits

Serves: 1

Ingredients:

- 2 cups Carbquik
- 2 oz. unsalted butter, cold
- 4 oz. shredded cheddar cheese
- ½ tsp. garlic powder

- ½ tsp. salt
- ¼ cup heavy cream
- ¼ cup water

Instructions:

1. Combine carbquik and chilled butter in a bowl. Add the butter pieces, and stir until the mixture resembles small pea-sized balls of flour and butter. Incorporate the cheese, salt, and garlic powder, blending thoroughly.

2. Stir in the water and heavy cream. Stir to form a dough. Divide into six pieces and arrange on a sheet that has been oiled. Bake them at 450°F for 8–10 minutes.

Nutritional Information:

Calories: 45

Net Carbs: 2.5g

Fat: 4g

Protein: 1.6g

Bacon Wrap

Serves: 4

Ingredients:

- 16 oz. beef
- 4 bacon slices
- Montreal steak seasoning

Instructions:

1. Season and cut the beef into cubes.

2. Slicing the bacon into four pieces.

3. After encasing the steak in bacon, puncture it with a toothpick. Do this twice or three times. Fry for three minutes.

Nutritional Information:

Calories: 217

Net Carbs: 0g

Fat: 10g

Protein: 30g

Sausage & Cabbage Skillet Melt

Serves: 4

Ingredients:

- 4 spicy Italian chicken sausages

- 1½ cups purple cabbage, shredded
- 1½ cups green cabbage, shredded
- ½ cup onion, diced 2 tsp. coconut oil
- tsp. fresh cilantro, chopped
- slices Colby jack cheese

Instructions:

1. Chop the onion and shred the cabbage (or use pre-shredded cabbage).

2. In a big skillet, melt the coconut oil and sauté the onion and cabbage. For eight minutes, cook on medium-high.

3. Stir the meat into the vegetables after adding it. Cook for an additional eight minutes.

4. Cover with the cheese after adding it.

5. While the cheese melts into the veggies, turn off the heat.

Nutritional Information:

Calories: 233

Net Carbs: 5g

Fat: 15g

Protein: 20g

Spaghetti Squash With Meat Sauce
Serves: 8

Ingredients:

- 2 spaghetti squashes
- 33-oz. jar of spaghetti sauce
- 2 lb. ground beef
- 1 tbsp. minced garlic
- Parmesan cheese
- 1 tbsp. Italian seasoning

Instructions:

1. Halve the spaghetti squash and remove the seeds. In a glass container half filled with water, cook the remaining shell and meat at 375°F for 45 minutes or until tender.

2. Over the heat, brown some meat. Stir in the sauce and seasonings. Warm up thoroughly.

3. After taking the cooked spaghetti squash out of the oven with care, make

spaghetti with a fork. Serve it dished with the sauce.

Nutritional Information:

Calories: 170

Net Carbs: 12g

Fat: 15g

Protein: 11g

Keto Chicken Tikka Masala

Serves: 5.

Ingredients:

- 1 lb. chicken thighs (boneless/skinless)
- 2 tsp. onion powder
- 2 tbsp. olive oil
- 3 minced garlic cloves
- 3 tbsp. tomato paste
- 1 inch grated ginger root
- tsp. garam masala
- 2 tsp. smoked paprika
- 10 oz. diced tomatoes (can)
- 4 tsp. kosher salt
- 1 cup coconut milk

- Fresh chopped cilantro 1 tsp. guar gum
- 1 cup heavy cream

Instructions:

1. Remove the chicken thighs' bones. Cut the chicken into small pieces with a knife.

2. Place the chicken in a slow cooker and sprinkle the ginger on top.

3. Combine the canned tomatoes and tomato paste with the remaining dry spices in a separate bowl. Add 1 cup coconut milk and stir. Include in the slow cooker.

4. Cook on high for three hours, or on low for six hours.

5. When done, stir in the guar gum, double cream, and remaining coconut milk. Blend.

Nutritional Information:

Calories: 495

Net Carbs: 5g

Fat: 43g

Protein: 25g

Keto Guacamole

Serves: 8

Ingredients:

- 4 avocados
- 2 tomatoes, chopped
- 1 small onion, chopped
- 1 tbsp. lime juice
- 1 jalapeño, chopped
- ½ tsp. cumin
- ½ tsp. salt
- ½ tsp. salt
- 1 tbsp. minced garlic
- ½ tsp. cayenne pepper

Instructions:

1. In a large bowl, combine the lime juice and the diced and skinned avocados. Using a potato masher, mash the avocados and add the spices.

2. Remix after adding the tomatoes, onions, and jalapenos.

3. Before serving, let it rest for one hour.

Nutritional Information:

Calories: 141

Net Carbs: 12g

Fat: 11g

Protein: 4g

Keto Parmesan Chicken

Serves: 4

Ingredients:

For the Chitken:

- 3 chicken breasts
- Salt and pepper
- 1 cup mozzarella cheese

For the Coating:

- ¼ cup flaxseed meal
- ½ cup parmesan cheese
- 2½ oz. pork rinds
- 1 tsp. oregano
- ½ tsp. pepper
- ½ tsp. salt
- ¼ tsp. red pepper flakes
- ½ tsp. garlic

- 1 egg
- 2 tsp. paprika
- 1½ tsp. chicken broth

The Saute

- 1 cup tomato sauce
- ¼ cup olive oil
- ½ tsp. garlic
- Salt and pepper
- ½ tsp. oregano

Instructions:

1. Grind the pork rinds, parmesan cheese, and spices in a food processor.

2. Season the chicken breasts with salt and pepper after slicing them into thirds.

3. To make the coating, whisk together the eggs and chicken stock in a separate basin.

4. Put all the sauce ingredients in a saucepan and whisk to combine. Start making the sauce. Simmer for 20 minutes.

5. To bread the chicken slices, first dunk them in the egg mixture and

subsequently in the coating made of pork rind. Place it on a foil-covered surface.

6. Heat a few tablespoons in a pan of olive oil, then sear the chicken. Transfer the chicken to a casserole dish and top with cheese and sauce. Bake at 400°F for 10 minutes.

Nutritional Information:

Calories: 646

Net Carbs: 5g

Fat: 47g

Protein: 49g

Cheesy Bacon Brussels Sprouts

Serves: 4

Ingredients:

- 5 slices bacon
- 6 oz. cheddar cheese
- 16 oz. Brussels sprouts

Instructions:

1. Fry the bacon to break it up. Chop into tiny fragments.

2. Use a food processor to finely chop the Brussels sprouts. Fry them in bacon oil until soft.

3. When the Brussels sprouts are transparent and crispy, add the cheese and bacon.

4. Heat through until melted.

Nutritional Information:

Calories: 260

Net Carbs: 5g

Fat: 22g

Protein: 17g

Creamy Chicken

Serves: 1.

Ingredients:

- 5 oz. chicken breast
- 3 oz. mushrooms
- 1 tbsp. olive oil
- ¼ small onion, sliced

- ¼ cup heavy cream
- ½ cup chicken broth
- ½ tsp. dried tarragon
- Salt and pepper
- 1 tsp. grain mustard

Instructions:

1. After cutting the chicken into cubes, season and oil-brown them. Take out and put on a platter.

2. In the same pan, add the mushrooms and sauté until browned. When the onion becomes transparent, add it and sauté it.

3. Pour in the chicken broth. Let it boil for three to five minutes to reduce.

4. Mix in the remaining ingredients and seasonings. Simmer for three to five more minutes after adding the chicken.

Nutritional Information:

Calories: 489

Net Carbs: 5g

Fat: 43g

Protein: 30g

Low Carb Chicken Nuggets

Serves: 4

Ingredients:

For the Nuggets:

- 1 egg
- 24 oz. chicken thighs

For the Crust:

- 1½ oz. pork rinds
- Zest of 1 lime
- ¼ cup almond meal
- ⅛ tsp. garlic powder
- ¼ cup flax meal
- ¼ tsp. paprika
- ⅛ tsp. onion powder
- ¼ tsp. chili powder
- ⅛ tsp. cayenne pepper
- ¼ tsp. pepper
- ¼ tsp. salt

For the Saute:

- ½ cup mayonnaise
- ¼ tsp. garlic powder
- ½ avocado
- 1 tbsp. lime juice

- ½ tsp. red chili flakes
- ⅛ tsp. cumin

Instructions:

1. After patting the chicken dry, chop it into small pieces.

2. Blend together all of the crust's ingredients in a food processor.

3. Place the crumbs in one basin and the whisked egg in another. Lay the chicken on a baking sheet that has been oiled after dipping it in the egg and crust. Bake at 400°F for 15 to 20 minutes.

4. Combine all of the sauce's ingredients to make the sauce.

Nutritional Information:

Calories: 615

Net Carbs: 2g

Fat: 53g

Protein: 39g

Cheeseburger Soup With Bacon

Serves: 5.

Ingredients:

- 5 slices bacon
- 2 tbsp. butter
- 12 oz. ground beef
- ½ tsp. garlic powder
- 3 cups beef broth
- ½ tsp. onion powder
- ½ tsp. red pepper flakes
- 2 tsp. brown mustard
- 1 tsp. chili powder
- 2½ tsp. tomato paste
- 1 tsp. cumin
- 1 medium dill pickle, diced
- 3 ounce cream cheese
- 1 cup shredded cheddar cheese
- ½ cup heavy cream
- ½ tsp. black pepper
- 1½ tsp. salt

Instructions:

1. In a frying pan, cook the bacon until crispy. Take out and break up into a little basin.

2. Brown the ground beef in the bacon grease that's left over.

3. Place the meat in a soup pot and add the spices and butter. Give the butter time to melt.

4. Add the pickles, cheese, tomato paste, and beef broth; heat until the cheese melts. After 20 more minutes of simmering at low heat, cover the pot.

5. After turning off the burner, stir in the double cream and bacon bits. Blend thoroughly.

Nutritional Information:

Calories: 573

Net Carbs: 4g

Fat: 48g

Protein: 24g

Sushie!

Serves: 3

Ingredients:

- 16 oz. cauliflower

- 1 tbsp. soy sauce
- 1-2 tbsp. unseasoned rice vinegar
- 6 oz. softened cream cheese
- 5 sheets nori
- ½ avocado
- 1-½-inch length of cucumber
- 5 oz. smoked salmon

Instructions:

1. Put the cauliflower in a food processor and rice it.

2. Each cucumber should be thinly sliced lengthwise. Store in the refrigerator until you need it.

3. In a heated pan, cook the cauliflower rice until it's almost soft. Add soy sauce for seasoning. Once cooked, combine with cream cheese and rice vinegar in a bowl and refrigerate until cool.

4. Slice the avocado thinly.

5. Arrange a sheet of nori on a bamboo roller. Cover practically the whole nori sheet with a layer of cauliflower. On one end, arrange the cucumber, avocado, and salmon. Roll firmly.

Nutritional Information:

Calories: 350

Net Carbs: 6g

Fat: 26g

Protein: 18g

Keto Salad With Radish And Asparagus

Serves: 4

Ingredients:

- 10 radishes
- 1½ lb. asparagus spears
- 4 oz. sour cream
- 1 tbsp. lemon juice
- 1 tbsp. dill
- 1 tsp. white wine vinegar
- 1 tbsp. mayonnaise
- 1 tsp. parsley
- 1 tbsp. olive oil
- Pepper

Instructions:

1. Put some salt in a kettle and bring the water to a boil. After washing the

asparagus stalks, trim the woody ends. When the required softness is reached, boil for two to three minutes after adding.

2. To stop the asparagus from cooking, put it in a kettle of ice water.

3. Remove the radishes' tops and bottoms, then thinly slice them.

4. Blend the remaining ingredients to make the dressing.

5. Toss to coat the asparagus, radishes, and dressing equally.

Nutritional Information:

Calories: 156

Net Carbs: 10g

Fat: 10g

Protein: 5g

Kung Pao Chicken

Serves: 3

Ingredients:

For the Chitken:

- 2 medium chicken thighs
- ¼ cup peanuts
- 1 tsp. ground ginger
- ½ green pepper
- 2 large spring onions
- 4 de-seeded red bird's eye chilies
- Salt and pepper

For the Saute:

- 1 tbsp. soy sauce
- 2 tsp. rice wine vinegar
- 2 tbsp. chili garlic paste
- 1 tbsp. reduced-sugar ketchup
- 2 tsp. sesame oil
- ½ tsp. maple extract
- 10 drops liquid stevia

Instructions:

1. Slice the chicken into little pieces and add ginger, salt, and pepper to taste.

2. In a pan over medium-high heat, cook the chicken until browned, about 10 minutes.

3. Mixing all the sauce components together will create the sauce.

4.Chop the chiles and veggies. Add all the ingredients and cook for an additional three to four minutes after the chicken is done. When the sauce is added, cook it until it reduces.

Nutritional Information:

Calories: 360

Net Carbs: 3g

Fat: 27.5g

Protein: 22g

Keto Totchos

Serves:2.

Ingredients:

- 2 servings keto tater tots
- 2 oz. shredded cheddar cheese
- 6 oz. ground beef
- 2 tbsp. sour cream
- 1 tbsp. salsa
- 6 sliced black olives
- ½ jalapeño pepper, sliced

Instructions:

1. In a small casserole pan, combine nine or ten keto tots and half of the ground meat and cheese. Layer the second layer of tots, then top with the remaining cheese and meat.

2. Serve with salsa, jalapenos, black olives, and sour cream. Broil for 5 minutes to melt the cheese.

Nutritional Information:

Calories: 638

Net Carbs: 6g

Fat: 53g

Protein: 32g

Stuffed Burgers

Serves: 2

Ingredients:

- 8 oz. ground beef
- ½ tsp. pepper
- 1 tsp. salt
- 1 tsp. Cajun seasoning
- 1 ounce mozzarella cheese
- 1 tbsp. butter

- 2 oz. cheddar cheese
- 2 slices pre-cooked bacon

Instructions:

1. Season the ground beef with Cajun seasoning, salt, and pepper. Press into a patty shape and stuff with mozzarella cheese. Once again, flatten and cover.

2. Heat one tablespoon of butter per burger in a pan. Add the burger and cook it for two to three minutes on each side. Add cheese, place a lid on it, and continue steaming for an additional two minutes.

3. Halve the bacon slices and place them on top.

Nutritional Information:

Calories: 615

Net Carbs: 1.5g

Fat: 50g

Protein: 35g

PORK PIES

Serves: 4

Ingredients:

- 1 lb. ground pork
- 2 beaten eggs
- ½ tbsp. grated parmesan cheese
- ½ tsp. ginger
- ½ tsp. ground nutmeg
- ½ lemon zest
- Salt and pepper
- ½ tsp. cardamom
- 4 tart shells (keto)

Instructions:

1. Put the meat and seasonings in a pan and heat it up. When it's just starting to cook, remove and stir in the egg and lemon.

2. Fill pie shells with some of the mixture, and bake for 20 to 25 minutes. Remove from the oven and allow to cool.

Nutritional Information:

Calories: 560

Net Carbs: 6g

Fat: 23g

Protein: 30g

Keto Thai Zoodles

Serves: 1.

Instructions:

- 3½ oz. chicken thighs
- 3½ oz. zucchini
- ½ tsp. curry powder
- 1 clove garlic
- 1 stalk spring onion
- ½ tsp. oyster sauce
- 1 tsp. soy sauce
- 1 tbsp. butter
- ⅛ tsp. white pepper
- 1 egg
- 1 tbsp. coconut oil
- 1 tsp. lime juice Chopped red chilies
- 1 ⅕ oz. bean sprouts
- Salt and pepper

Instructions:

1. To marinate the chicken, add salt, pepper, and curry powder.

2. To make the zoodles, slice the zucchini into extremely thin strips. Dice the garlic and onion into tiny pieces.

3. Combine the oyster sauce, white pepper, and soy sauce to make the sauce.

4. Once the chicken is browned and sliced into little pieces, cook it in butter.

5. Add the coconut oil to the same pan over high heat and sauté the garlic and onion. Cook the egg until it begins to take on some color.

6. Stir in the zoodles and bean sprouts. Stir in the chicken after adding the sauce and mixing.

7. Add some chopped red chilies and lemon juice as garnish.

Nutritional Information:

Calories: 581

Net Carbs: 7g

Fat: 50g

Protein: 26g

Chicken Satay

Serves: 3

Ingredients:

- 4 tbsp. soy sauce
- 1 lb. ground chicken
- 3 tbsp. peanut butter
- 1 tbsp. rice vinegar
- 1 tbsp. erythritol
- 2 tsp. sesame oil
- 1 tsp. minced garlic
- 2 tsp. chili paste
- ¼ tsp. cayenne
- ¼ tsp. paprika
- ½ tsp. lime juice
- 2 chopped spring onions
- ⅓ sliced yellow pepper

Instructions:

1. Place the sesame oil in a skillet over medium-high heat and fry the ground chicken. Mix thoroughly after adding the remaining ingredients.

2. Once cooked, stir in the yellow pepper and onions, then serve.

Nutritional Information:

Calories: 395

Net Carbs: 4g

Fat: 24g

Protein: 35g

Stuffed Peppers

Serves: 1

Ingredients:

- 1 lb. ground pork
- 4 poblano peppers
- 1 tsp. chili powder
- 1 tbsp. bacon fat
- ½ onion 1 tomato
- 7 baby bella mushrooms
- Salt and pepper
- ¼ cup packed cilantro
- 1 tsp. cumin

Instructions:

1. In the oven, broil the poblano peppers for around 8 to 10 minutes.

2. Pork is browned in bacon grease. Add chile, cumin, salt, and pepper for seasoning.

3. Add the minced garlic and chopped onion. Combine all ingredients and stir in the sliced mushrooms. Add the tomato and chopped cilantro after they've absorbed all of the grease in the pan. Simmer for a period of 12 minutes.

4. After filling the peppers, bake at 350° for 8 minutes.

Nutritional Information:

Calories: 368

Net Carbs: 6g

Fat: 27g

Protein: 22g

Coconut Shrimp

Serves: 3.

Ingredients:

For the Coconut Shrimp:

- 1 lb. peeled and de-veined shrimp
- 1 cup unsweetened coconut flakes
- 2 egg whites
- 2 tbsp. coconut flour

For the Sweet Chili Dipping Saute:

- ½ cup sugar free apricot preserves
- 1 tbsp. lime juice
- ½ tsp. rice wine vinegar
- ¼ tsp. red pepper flakes
- 1 medium diced red chili

Instructions:

1. The egg whites should be beaten until soft peaks form. Divide the coconut flour and flakes into two separate bowls.

2. The shrimp are dipped in egg whites, coconut flakes, and coconut flour in order of preference. Put the shrimp on a baking sheet that has been oiled. Bake for fifteen minutes at 400°F. Flip and broil for three to five minutes, or until browned and crispy.

3. Combine all the dipping sauce components to make the sauce.

Nutritional Information:

Calories: 398

Net Carbs: 7g

Fat: 22g

Protein: 36g

Glazed Salmon

Serves: 2

Ingredients:

- 10 oz. salmon filet
- 2 tsp. sesame oil
- 2 tbsp. soy sauce
- 1 tbsp. rice vinegar
- 2 tsp. garlic minced
- 1 tsp. ginger, minced
- 1 tbsp. red boat fish sauce
- 1 tbsp. sugar free ketchup
- 2 tbsp. white wine

Instructions:

1. Marinate the salmon for ten to fifteen minutes in a jar with all of the ingredients (except for the ketchup, sesame oil, and white wine).

2. Skin side down, lay the filet in a pan over high heat with a little sesame oil added until it starts to smoke.

3. Cook for 4 minutes on each side, or until crisp on all sides. To make the glaze, remove the fish.

4. To the marinade, add white wine and ketchup. Add to the pan and simmer until reduced to a glaze, about 5 minutes.

Nutritional Information:

Calories: 372

Net Carbs: 3g

Fat: 24g

Protein: 35g

Conclusion

We thus close the recipe book! What was it like? Have you found the recipes to be simple? The ketogenic diet seems intimidating. First of all, the instant you start and develop it into a habit, you will notice how easily the novice in you could do it. Beginning with breakfast, lunch, supper, and snacks, the meals were created with exact Instructions to satisfy ketogenic diet criteria.

Not only that, but you have also learned about how the ketogenic diet works, along with its hazards and advantages, some fantastic ideas and practices to help you, and a list of simple and enjoyable meals to cook.

Regarding the recipes, this book reveals that many of your preferred foods and snacks have been developed to be ketogenic.

You also perused recipes you never would have imagined could be created. Recipes for the ketogenic diet allow you to see food from a whole new perspective.

The contents of this book will enable you to start your ketogenic diet with assurance. So finish it, test the dishes, and have fun!

Printed in Great Britain
by Amazon